THE HEAD
WEARS A CROWN

POEMS ABOUT KINGS AND QUEENS

ACKNOWLEDGEMENTS

'Queen Maeve Rules!', 'Conn of the Hundred Battles' and 'The Brian Boru Burger', by Alan Murphy, were first published in *All Gums Blazing* (AvantCard Publications) in 2018.

THE EMMA PRESS

First published in the UK in 2018 by the Emma Press Ltd.

Poems © individual copyright holders 2018
Selection © Rachel Piercey and Emma Dai'an Wright 2018

ISBN 978-1-910139-76-9

A CIP catalogue record of this book
is available from the British Library.

Printed and bound in the EU by Pulsio, Paris.

The Emma Press
theemmapress.com
hello@theemmapress.com
Jewellery Quarter, Birmingham, UK

THE HEAD THAT WEARS A CROWN

POEMS ABOUT KINGS AND QUEENS

Edited by Rachel Piercey and Emma Dai'an Wright

With notes by Rachel Piercey and Richard O'Brien

Introduction

I have wanted to help edit an anthology on kings and queens ever since the Emma Press started publishing books for children. As a child, I loved Eleanor and Herbert Farjeon's poems about kings and queens, and their funny, dashing character studies helped me remember lots of details about the lives of British monarchs.

Loved or loathed, kings and queens have intrigued writers since the earliest times and I wanted to be part of a book where these fierce, flawed, fascinating figures were once more brought to life.

Whatever you think about the role of the monarchy – and people have lots of different opinions – the laws, beliefs and actions of these rulers have shaped our history, and it helps us understand our current society to learn about them.

The brilliant poets in this book have written about monarchs who ruled over a period of 2,000 years, with poems in a range of different styles. Some poems are funny, some are lyrical; some are sympathetic, some are critical; but they all give us a vivid insight into lives very different from our own.

The book is full of rich details from different periods of time and the poets have had great fun with their research. We've also added some notes where we thought it would be helpful to know more about the historical context. But it's important to remember that these are dramatic, poetic interpretations rather than factual texts. If you are interested in a particular king, queen or era, then enjoy researching them yourself!

The title of our anthology, 'The Head that Wears a Crown', is a quotation from Shakespeare's play *Henry IV, Part II*. The full line is

'Uneasy lies the head that wears a crown' and King Henry is making the point that kingship is a mixed blessing, which brings great responsibility and stress as well as wealth and power. Shakespeare wrote lots of plays about kings and queens and they have influenced the way we think about these figures.

Indeed, lots of history is made up of stories people have told and written down rather than cold, hard facts. It's useful to do lots of reading around a subject to get a rounded look at any given person or period. Many of the poems in the book explore this idea, looking at the way we study history and historical characters, how these stories are passed down to us, and how much we can say for certain about the past.

One thing we *can* say for certain is that the kings and queens of Britain and Ireland make for an extremely lively, quirky cast of characters. These monarchs start rebellions, burn cakes, steal bulls, purloin crowns, battle with their siblings, plot takeovers, go wild with power, haunt castles, escape to exile and often come to sticky ends. We hope you enjoy meeting them… just try to keep your head!

Rachel Piercey
NOVEMBER 2018

• •

NOTE: We've included dates and titles for the monarchs at the bottom of each page, but it's worth noting that, at different points in history, the ruler of England also made claims to power over Ireland and parts of France. The status of Wales as a separate nation has also been disputed throughout British history. In this book, we are using titles that make the clearest sense to modern day readers, which sometimes gloss over these important historical complexities.

• •

Contents

BONUS BITS

WHO MADE THIS BOOK?

Most of the early legends about
King Arthur place him in the
6th century AD. Historians
don't really know when this
monarch ruled, largely because
they don't believe he existed.

Untitled

Richard O'Brien

One English king is ringed
in mystery: Arthur.
Real monarchs need full poems.
He gets half a

··········

Arthur

1

Queen Maeve Rules!

Alan Murphy

Queen of Connacht and Goddess Supreme,
the boldest woman Eire's ever seen.
Queen Maeve rules!

Strong-willed, ambitious, cunning, alluring,
powerful, amorous, deadly and daring.
Queen Maeve rules!

Married to Ailill mac Máta one day,
over all Connacht their firm rule held sway.
Queen Maeve rules!

....

Maeve (Medb)
Queen of Connacht, Ireland

And short of a stud bull she hatched a shrewd plan –
to beg / borrow / steal one from some other land.
Queen Maeve rules!

Dáire mac Fiachna's most suitable beast
was strutting in Cooley way off in the east.
Queen Maeve Rules!

So, hiring the help of some exiles from Ulster,
Maeve sent every warrior that she could muster.
Queen Maeve rules!

The cattle raid seemed at first sure of success,
as the cursed, unmanned district was in great distress.
Queen Maeve rules!

So teenage Cuchulainn alone held the ford:
his war fury routed the treacherous horde.
Queen Maeve rules!

But in spite of Cuchulainn the bull was secured
before a retreat of Maeve's overwhelmed curs.
Queen Maeve Rules!

Though the animal's new life – alas! – came to nil:
it died of its wounds, fighting mac Mata's bull.
Queen Maeve rules!

And speaking of endings, Maeve's own was a wheeze.
She was killed by a slingshot containing some cheese.
Queen Maeve rules!

Now Irish place names keep Queen Maeve on the map:
Maeve's hill, Maeve's knoll, Maeve's hut and Maeve's gap.
Queen Maeve rules!

And her tale's since regaled every Tom, Dick and Michael,
wherever folk peddle the Ulster Cycle.
Queen Maeve rules!

. . . .
Like King Arthur,
Queen Maeve is a
legendary figure and no
one is sure of the truth
of her story or the
dates of her reign.
. . . .

. . . .
She is meant to have
ruled Connacht, a
province of Ireland, in
the west of the country.
(Eire is the Irish name
for Ireland.)
. . . .

. . . .
Queen Maeve's cattle raid,
known as the Táin Bó
Cúailnge, is the longest
story in the Ulster Cycle, a
collection of Irish medieval
mythological tales.
. . . .

4

From Boudicca, Queen of the Iceni, to Gaius Suetonius Paullinus, on the occasion of his invasion

Kirsten Irving

'In stature she was very tall, in appearance most terrifying, in the glance of her eye most fierce...'
Cassius Dio, Roman historian

Governor! Well, what an honour –
visiting wee, cold Britannia!
Come and sit down by the fire.
Let me tell you how it works here.

. . . .

Boudicca
Queen of British Celtic Iceni tribe, middle of the 1st century AD

Take a leg of roasted ewe.
Take a cup of steaming stew.
Take a tour and take the view.
Take your cloak off, and your shoes.

Take our lands and take our stars.
Take our jewellery, coins and furs.
Take our plough and take our horse.
Take our children from their mothers.

Take a dagger to your throat.
Take an arrow to your heart.
Take my short sword to your gut.
Take the hint, Gaius. Get out.

Boudicca, a fearsome warrior
queen, led a rebellion in AD 60
or 61 against the Roman troops
who had invaded Britain. She was
eventually defeated but she has
always been seen as a great hero.

The last semi-mythical
monarch in this book,
Conn is most commonly
claimed to have ruled in
the 2nd century AD.

Conn of the Hundred Battles

Alan Murphy

On the occasion
of his final skirmish,
High King Conn,
AKA Conn of the Hundred Battles,
was done in
by Tipraite Tirech,
king of the Ulaid.

You can't help feeling
he would have been fine
if he'd left it at ninety-nine.

Conn of the Hundred Battles
High King of Ireland

Egbert

Richard O'Brien

So now, hear this – there's seven kings
(who ever heard of such a thing?)
who shared the land in 802.
        When I say 'shared', I mean like you
        might share this book with younger siblings:
calmly first, then some slight quibbling,
then a touch of quibbling more,
then screaming, fighting, all-out war,
tearing out pages, clumps of hair:
that's what the Saxons meant by 'share'.

....

Ecgberht
King of Wessex, 802 - 839, with periods as King of Kent,
Surrey, Sussex, Essex, and Mercia after 826

When seven Saxons ruled the country
(some say more, but seven's plenty)
no one ruler could move forwards –
not with six whole other warlords.
       Kent, East Anglia, and Wessex,
       Sussex, Mercia, and Essex,
and Northumbria – all seven
thought their little slice was Heaven,
but would still invade each other's.
On they fought, like squabbling brothers

– all of them, of course, were men –
won, then lost, then won again
their well-loved little patch of turf.
With swords and gold, they rest in earth.
       But, through history's dark fog,
       one man became the biggest dog
in battle. This meant many died
who had no stake in either side,
but good or bad, King Egbert won
against Beornwulf at Ellandun,

in Wiltshire. It's quite calm today –
it's got a picturesque café –
but where you clink your cups and spoons
the soldiers' blood was on the dunes.
       The King of Wessex beat the Mercians –
       not because they were the worst ones,

just because – and so became
the leader with the widest reign.
They named him Britain's King: 'Bretwalda'.
(Hope he called his Mum and told her!)

King from Kent to Cornwall's borders.
Hard to keep it all in order
from the East across to Wales;
but they told of him in tales:

Bretwalda,   *first boss of Britain,*
Egbert endured.   *It wasn't easy,*
keeping the kingdom   *calm. The Cornish*
fought him   *fiercely and often.*
No mean feat   *to unite a nation*
(although it fell apart   *soon after) –*
he helped make   *the Heptarchy history.*
Who was his wife?   *Well, that's a mystery.*

You might also see King Egbert's name spelt Ecgberht or Ecgbryht – it's common to see different versions of old names because for many centuries people didn't worry much about standardised spelling.

Sometimes people also modernise the names to make them easier to spell and pronounce. You'll see some different versions of royal names throughout the book.

While modern poetry can rhyme (although it doesn't have to), Old English poetry never did. Instead, it alliterated. That is, several words in each line start with similar sounds.

Because it was all meant to be performed aloud to music, these similar sounds gave it a powerful rhythm. Richard has used this form in the last verse of his poem.

11

King Alfred's burnt cakes: probably the most famous baking disaster in history! Did it really happen? We'll probably never know – the first written version of the tale, that we know of, dates from around two hundred years after the supposed charring.

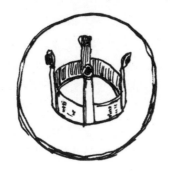

King Alfred's Dream

Jeremy Wikeley

King Alfred is hungry.
He's on the run from the Vikings,
hiding in a swineherd's hut
on an island in the middle of a lake
in Somerset.

'We've been running for years!'
he tells the swineherd's wife.
She's not impressed.
She's half-expecting tears.

Alfred the Great
King of the Anglo-Saxons, 871 - 899

12

'I suppose if you watch those
cakes while I go out
then you can have one or two
of them later,' she says,
pointing to a few lumps of flour by the fire.
'Just one thing, Alfred,
King of England...

don't you dare burn them!'

In many versions of the
story, the cake-baking
woman has no idea that
Alfred is king.

Outside spring was waking up.
The morning was misty and wet.
Alfred sat back
and dreamed of England.

He dreamed
all his fields were covered in buildings
with nobody living there,
just pairs of emerald pigeons
flitting between them.

He dreamed
there was a candle the size of a cathedral
and all the townspeople
were huddled around it,
on a cold night,
with a thousand faces in the crowd
behind them and the faces
stretched away into the gloom
further and further,
each face getting colder
and colder...

He dreamed
of silver ships sailing through the clouds,
and all their passengers were
dressed in gold.
He dreamed so long his feet got cold.

He dreamed
of a thousand voices shouting
You've burnt the cakes! You've burnt the cakes,
for God's sake Alfred,
you've burnt the cakes!

He dreamed
he heard a flock of geese
landing on the lake

and woke up with a jolt.

The fire had burnt out.
There was no one there.

Alfred put the cakes in his bag,
left a coin on the seat
and rowed back across the lake
to Wiltshire.

• • • • • • • • • • • • • • • • • • •

After leaving Somerset,
Alfred moved on to
Wiltshire for the Battle of
Edington, where his army
was victorious against the
Vikings.

• • • • • •

A short rhyme
for a short reign:
Ælfweard

Jerrold Bowam

Long may Ælfweard
reign, they prayed,

but in two weeks
he'd passed away.

They prayed again;
Æthelstan,
long may he reign.

....

Ælfweard of Wessex
King of Wessex, 17th July 924 - 2nd August 924

When Edward the Elder died, his kingdoms of Wessex and Mercia were split between two of his sons. Ælfweard took power in Wessex, but only lived for sixteen days – his brother, Æthelstan, then ended up ruling both kingdoms.

After conquering Northumbria, Æthelstan signed a peace treaty with Welsh and Scottish kings at Eamont (near Penrith) and started issuing coins calling himself 'King of the whole of Britain'.

The average life expectancy for a man at this time was 38.2 years (for women it was 35.8, probably because women often died in childbirth). Kings had easier lives than the average Anglo-Saxon and no shortage of food and drink. Despite this, the average age for a king was also 38.

Æthelstan

Jennifer Watson

Æthelstan, what a star!
Yet no one now knows who you are.
Your ruling hand, both firm and fair,
held sword and pen with equal flair.
Minter of coins and maker of rules,
administering justice, punishing fools.
Righter of wrongs, you made no mistakes –
I'll bet you're a man who didn't burn cakes.
Æthelstan, it's such a shame
that Grandad Alfred stole your fame.

....

Æthelstan
King of the Anglo-Saxons, 924 - 927
King of the English, 927 - 939

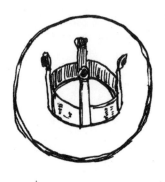

Your Elfrida

Anna Kisby

Seven-feet tall, I am Queen of your dreams.
Lady of stained-glass, robed in purple folds.
My slaves weave miles of cloth until my body
turns to heather-fields.

West Country queen, inside me lives
the memory of giants forming these hills.
Fair as tin, I glint like sunlight on your streams.
I outwit any man at games of chess, or death.

·············

Ælfthryth
Queen Consort of England, 964 - 975

Edgar I
King of England, 959 - 975

Wife, Mother, Grandmother of Kings,
I am a rider of stallions, strong as these rocks but
I like to remember what it is to be soft.
I wear blue fur against my skin.

Queen of nuns, I give women a small walled place
to be almost-free, to write their way into history.
For a while I rule your land, sign my name.
Until the tongues begin their dog-tail wags.

My golden crown is plundered, or in particles,
lost, long melted-down.
So you may find me, and know me real,
I leave my long thigh-bones behind.

Elfrida (or Ælfthryth),
wife of King Edgar, was
the first crowned Queen
of England, in 973.

Purple dye was so rare and
costly to make (it came from
the mucus of tiny sea snails!)
that it was always associated
with royalty and riches.

Many medieval stories
blamed Elfrida for the
murder of her stepson,
King Edward the Martyr.

Æthelred was one of Elfrida's sons. He may have been as young as nine when he came to the throne after King Edward's murder.

Æthelred the Unready

Kate O'Neil

Time has come to set it down:
my name was not 'Unready'.
I might have been a little green,
I might have been unsteady,
but think! I wasn't yet a teen –
far too young to wear a crown.

The thing is, I was 'ill-advised':
that's Æthelred 'Unræd'.
All I knew of being King
was doing things that others said.
This error is a hurtful thing –
please have your books revised.

Æthelred the Unready
King of England, 978 - 1013, 1014 - 1016

One explanation of Brian's nickname in the Irish language, 'Bóruma', is that it means 'Brian of the cattle tribute'. Kings were often honoured by their subjects through payments of livestock.

Brian's Saga

Jennifer Watson

Brian Boru was the boldest and best:
High King of Ireland, he awed and impressed.
Focus of fable and subject of song,
his shoulders were broad and his shadow was long.

Brian of the Tributes! Rock of Cashel!
His cattle were many – his wives were as well.
There was Echrad, Dub Choblaig, Gormflaith and Mór
(when you tallied them up, then they came in at four).

His muscles were iron, his justice was swift:
Boru was a legend and soon became myth.
From Munster to Leinster he leapt with a bound
that parted the rivers and sundered the ground.

Brian Boru
King of Munster, 978 - 1014
High King of Ireland, 1002 - 1014

His failings were few and his fan base increased,
his cattle pens grew as his rivals deceased.
With one hand he sowed, with the other he slew,
like a storm from the South blew in Brian Boru.

On the high hill at Tara, his hand touched the Stone
and the Kingdom of Ireland was Brian's alone,
for the Stone cried, 'The prophecy now has come true
and destined for great things is Brian Boru!'

Life looked quite sunny, the prospects set fair,
Brian's foes were cast down in the depths of despair.
There were none who could match him, none fit in his shoes,
no footprint was bigger than Brian Boru's.

Now Ireland was finding some Vikings quite troublin'
so Boru got his boys and they marched down to Dublin.
Sigtrygg the Silkbeard he crushed with a zeal
(though he married his mother to sweeten the deal).

Those Norsemen were tricky and they sent out more orders
to bring reinforcements to aid the marauders.
They battled at Clontarf – a bloody affair –
the field ran with gore and the crows filled the air.

The Vikings were vanquished! The victory won!
But Brian Boru lost his life and his son.
He gave up the ghost as he prayed in his tent,
axed by a Viking who preyed with intent.

Hibernia is the Latin
name for Ireland.

The Brian Boru Burger

Alan Murphy

In bygone times
a bearded bloke
called Brian Boru
broke all the rules
by becoming
head bigwig
of badass
Hibernia.

Before too long
the poor boy
bit the dust
with a broadsword blow
on the battlefield.
Boo-hoo!

But a Dublin beerhouse
boldly broadcasts

Brian Boru
King of Munster, 978 - 1014
High King of Ireland, 1002 - 1014

his butch moniker
on its brickwork facade,
while his noble likeness
embarks triumphant
both front and side
on bonny horseback:
    burnished shield
    and blood red cape
    blowing in the breeze,
    what ebullience!

And the barman within
had another brainwave:

He beheld that
a burger bearing
the Brian Boru brand
might brew
a number one
banquet.
It did, by God.

Buttressed with chips
and vegetables,
the assembled object
is big as a bear.

It tastes brilliant,
                beguiling,
                    beauteous,
        beyond doubt
    truly ambrosial.

Brian who (it's boasted)
gave the Vikings a drubbing,
banished the invaders,
was tabbed by God…

Unmistakably
each bite contains
pure Irish blarney.

The Brian Boru Burger,
a blithe thing,
the brave boss of Ireland
a burger king!

Alan is using a different
version of Brian Boru's
death to Jennifer; here Brian
dies in battle. There are
lots of different stories told
about Brian's last hours.

The Witan was the king's
advisory council. This poem,
like 'Egbert' earlier, uses
alliteration in tribute to the
poetry of the time.

Back over in England, Vikings
were still causing havoc.
Danegeld was a tax imposed
by the king to strengthen the
English army, by paying for
extra soldiers.

Sweyn Forkbeard

J H Rice

Æthelred, the ill-advised,
tired of torment, drained of Danegeld.
Æthelred, led by the Witan,
took to carnage, wanton killing.

Warriors he slew: laid waste by sword!
Fair Gunhilde of flaxen hair,
sister to Sweyn, born of Bluetooth,
Gunhilde's life was not spared.

Sweyn Forkbeard, King of Denmark!
Sweyn Forkbeard, father's ruin!
Sweyn Forkbeard, in shining fury,
set his fleet to wreak revenge!

Sweyn Forkbeard
King of Denmark, 986 - 1014
King of Norway, 986 - 995
King of England, 1013 - 1014

Through the Humber, mudflats flashing.
Traced the river's winding waters.
Through the Trent, with whispered oar strokes,
prowled the long ships: swift to slaughter.

Sweyn Forkbeard took his tribute!
Held to hostage, boroughs bowed.
Blank-eyed dragons hewn from ships' prows
observed the victors, London bound.

Æthelred! Flee to exile!
Away to Wiht-land, thence to North-men.
Now sing to Sweyn, the King of England –
fallen breathless, two moons hence.

His son, Cnut, was briefly
named king by the Vikings,
but the Anglo-Saxons recalled·
Æthelred from exile and
made him king again. ·

Sweyn Forkbeard died
only a few weeks after
becoming king of England.

Æthelred ruled for two years, but
after he died and then his son
Edmund died, Cnut took over
the whole kingdom once more.
Complicated or what?

I, Canute!

Jane Burn

Son of the Forkbeard, I. Canute!
Tall and handsome – a good strong brute.
But for my nose, I would be cute –
hooked as a claw, long as a flute.
Two hundred longships make pursuit,
ten thousand warriors in cahoots.
We come with drum and cow's horn toot –
ten thousand strong and keen recruits!
Our feet are stood in good strong boots,
our shields are gold, our pants are jute.
We are muscle. We are hirsute.
We come for war – to spear and shoot.
I come to rule! I come to loot!
I come to plunder England's fruit!
I come to chuck your Ironside oot!
Be thou afraid! I am en route.
Son of the Forkbeard, I. Canute!
I wish to be of great repute –
to be considered most astute.

• • • • • • • • • • • • • • • • • •
People spell Canute's
name in lots of
different ways: Canute,
Cnut or Knut.
• • • • • • • • • • • •

• • • • • • • • • • • • •

Cnut the Great
King of England, 1016 - 1035
King of Denmark, 1018 - 1035
King of Norway, 1028 - 1035

If flattery is left to root,
a court will thrive in disrepute.
I'll show how I have stayed acute,
shall show how vanity pollutes,
how next to heaven we are minute
and wisdom is what it is all aboot –
no matter who, the sea commutes
both ways. The tide does not salute
or bow to kings, will not be cooped,
will not avoid a ruler's foot.
Foolish to test this absolute –
you will get wet, there is no doot.
Son of the Forkbeard, resolute.
Son of the Forkbeard, I. Canute!

There's a famous story about Cnut failing to hold back the tide, which people often use when they're making a point about someone being arrogant or deluded: 'He thought he could hold back the tide!'

However, in the original written version of the story, Cnut is deliberately showing his courtiers that he *can't* influence the waves, because he is not God but a mere mortal man. People love to tell stories and a powerful tale can take on a life of its own.

Knut

Melanie Branton

King Knut of Denmark was k-nown for daring feats.
He was Danish as a pastry, but nothing like as sweet.
You'd have weed in your k-nickers if you'd seen him in the street:
he was big and butch and burly and he had a mean repute.
Knut! Knut! Knut!

He could colonise all countries and then show them what was what!
You could go and get k-notted if you thought that he could not!
When Knut's k-nights convened, they gave it everything they'd got!
They conquered foreign lands and brought home lots of lovely loot!
Knut! Knut! Knut!

Knut set off for England, his k-napsack on his back.
He k-new that he could do it, as he just had the k-nack,
enough kinetic energy to pillage and to sack.
He cornered old King Æthelred and then stuck in the boot.
Knut! Knut! Knut!

Though Æthelred Unready had quickly been dispensed,
he had a son called Edmund, who was feeling quite incensed.
The story's convoluted, so I'll give it you condensed:
Knut confronted Edmund's troops and routed them en route.
Knut! Knut! Knut!

....

Cnut the Great
King of England, 1016 - 1035
King of Denmark, 1018 - 1035
King of Norway, 1028 - 1035

Knut was not contented with k-nowledge of his fame
(though he must have been k-nackered after battle, just the same).
He sought a prudent marriage to consolidate his claim,
to make quite sure the chance of deposition was minute.
Knut! Knut! Knut!

He made some swift advances and quite soon was going steady
with the very lovely widow of King Æthelred Unready.
They married in the summer, though he had a wife already –
and people thought this odd, but he just didn't give a hoot!
Knut! Knut! Knut!

When he reached the age of forty and his beard had grown
     canescent,
Knut fell ill with jaundice, which must have been unpleasant,
and confused them all by dying when they thought him
     convalescent,
so then his kingdom fell apart: it all went down the chute!
Knut! Knut! Knut!

. . . .
The Anglo-Saxons and
Vikings had common
ancestors who came from
the same place. This means
that their languages were
very similar but had drifted
apart over time.
. . . .

. . . .
When the Vikings settled
in the north of England
they brought new words
with new sounds, one of
which was 'K'.
. . . .

Brotherly Love: Harthacanute speaks out

Kate O'Neil

My brother, Harold Harefoot,
did the dirt on me.
When our father, King Canute,
died quite suddenly,
misbegotten Harold
claimed our father's crown,
while I, the heir legitimate,
was fighting out of town.
So with my Danish army
I planned to set things right
and headed home to England
raring for a fight.
But Harold, lousy lowlife,
chickened out and died
just before I got there –
he really had a hide.
So, since I couldn't kill him
I did the next best thing.

. . . .

Harthacnut
King of England, 1040 - 1042
King of Denmark, 1035 - 1042

I dug him up, removed his head,
then took the phony king
and flung him in the river.
At last the crown was mine –
and though I didn't keep it long
my triumph was Divine.

Remember Cnut's two
wives? Harold was the son
of Cnut's first wife, Ælfgifu
of Northampton, whilst
Harthacanute (or Harthacnut)
was the son of his second wife,
Emma of Normandy. The half-
brothers both believed they had
the right to the throne.

On Cnut's death,
Harthacnut got caught up
defending Denmark and
couldn't make it back in
time to claim his crown.

Many monarchs believed that
their power came from God
and gave them special status,
so they didn't have to answer
to any other human beings. In
later centuries, this concept
would come to be known as
the 'divine right of kings'.

Gruffydd ap Llywelyn was
the only Welsh ruler to
be recognised as King of
the whole of Wales.

The First and Last

Matthew Haigh

Many men wore my steel in their warm flesh.

I had rivals, true. Enemies?
I made a few.

To win hearts I had to sever heads,
so with my blade
I ran them through.

I took a castle in my palm,
crushed it like a snowflake's spur. Herefordshire fell.

Gruffydd ap Llywelyn
King of Wales, 1055 - 1063

All the country's corners I seized
with no more effort than a sneeze
and all recognised me
as King of Wales.

Seven years I reigned – time flew as fast
as an apple's tumble to grass.

Death swiped for me once, missed. Caught up with me
in Snowdonia.
A man called Cynan killed me
because I'd killed his father.

Hot blood in fog.

Who knows who won the prize of my lopped-off
head, with staring eyes full of sky?

Hear the soft slush of my name on the waves:
Gruffydd ap Llywelyn

a one-time-only King.

After Gruffydd ap Llywelyn's
death, the country was once
more split into separate
kingdoms with different rulers.

Both his head and the
figurehead of his ship
were sent to the Anglo-
Saxon King of England,
Harold Godwineson.

When Edward
the Confessor
died with no heir,
Harold Godwineson
and William of
Normandy both
claimed they had
been promised the
crown. This led
to the Battle of
Hastings in 1066.

Song of King Harold's Soldier

Jack Houston

Our feet, our feet, they don't half hurt.
We're tired, battle-worn and beat.
Our feet, our feet, they don't half hurt.
From York to Hastings in two weeks.

We've just been through one and here
comes another. How many skulls
will we have to crush before we can sit
and have a rest? My axe-arm aches.

Harold II (Harold Godwineson)
King of England, 5th January 1066 - 14th October 1066

Our feet, our feet, they don't half hurt.
We're tired, battle-worn and beat.
Our feet, our feet, they don't half hurt.
From York to Hastings, what a feat!

Mud, mud, mud, there's always mud
when marching. Our boots churn it up.
They're good and sturdy though, at least.
You wouldn't want them leaking.

Our feet, our feet, they don't half hurt.
We're tired, hungry and half-beat.
Our feet, our feet, they don't half hurt.
From York to Hastings in two weeks.

But I feel as fierce as chicken feed.
I'm not sure I want war at all. The fear,
the blood, the screams and worse.
I wouldn't wish it upon my enemies!

Our feet, our feet, they don't half hurt.
We're tired, hungry and half-beat.
Our feet, our feet, they don't half hurt.
From York to Hastings, what a feat!

I wouldn't and nor should you. But still,
we're here now on this southern hill.
We'll kill all these new invaders too.
My shield's as sure as I am.

Harold Godwineson and
his army fought the Battle
of Stamford Bridge in 1066
against the Norwegian king
Harald Hardrada and Harold
G's own brother, Tostig.

Harold G was victorious,
but had to travel south
immediately afterwards for the
Battle of Hastings, where he
and his army were defeated.

Harold's is one of the most famous
kingly deaths in history – but
historians aren't sure whether
the arrow shown in the Bayeux
Tapestry (an incredible artwork
which depicts the events leading
up to and including the Battle of
Hastings) is really even an arrow.

It might originally have been
a lance or a spear, which was
made to look more like an
arrow when the fabric was
repaired many centuries later.

The Ballad of Hastings

Elli Woollard

Harold made haste to Hastings,
marching on muck-mottled lanes,
Harold made haste to Hastings,
in pattering splattering rains.
With an army of men, a few thousand strong,
he trampled and stampled and pounded along.
Harold made haste to Hastings,
through fields and forests and plains.

Harold II (Harold Godwineson)
King of England, 5th January 1066 - 4th October 1066

The soldiers all raced to Hastings,
their footsteps resounding thud-thud,
the soldiers all raced to Hastings,
churning and turning up mud.
And there were the French, with William the Norman,
a mail-wearing, shield-bearing conquering war man.
The soldiers all raced to Hastings,
tasting the tang of spilled blood.

The armies laid waste to Hastings,
a furious axe-clanging clash,
the armies laid waste to Hastings,
a sword-swinging, spear-stinging smash,
till an arrow that pierced through the back of his eye
caused Harold the king to fall down and die.
The armies laid waste to Hastings,
and the sky was as cold as old ash.

And now if you're based near Hastings,
that blood-sodden, mud-trodden hill,
now if you're based near Hastings,
where soldiers stepped up to the kill,
on a long silent night, you might hear the ring
of the steel in the sword and the heart of that king.
Now if you're based near Hastings,
maybe you'll see his ghost still.

Christmas Day, 1066

Kirsten Irving

Merry Christmas, darling wife.
I got you an England to go with your France!
Yes, it's cold, and they've no sense of style
but you should see these Britons dance!

I've had a minstrel write a song
about my rather heroic skirmish.
People dying, arrows flying!
(It works in Norman and in English.)

....

William I (William the Conqueror)
Duke of Normandy, 1035 - 1087
King of England, 1066 - 1087

William was
crowned king in
Westminster Abbey
on Christmas Day.

No one knows who
made the Bayeux
Tapestry, but one
romantic legend holds
that it was William's
wife, Matilda.

Did the shipment reach you safely?
Silver, furs, a ton of clothes,
How-To scrolls on Tapestry...
(I don't know what you'll make of those.)

I wish you'd come to see the new place.
Harold's castle is very fine!
Bring Richard, Robert and all the rest.
And darling, bring some decent wine.

William

Maybe William II was
murdered, but it's far more
likely to have been a simple
hunting accident. William's
elder brother and nephew
both died in a similar manner.

Maybe it was just as
dangerous to be a king
in the New Forest as
to be a deer...

King William II

Dharmavadana

No one remembers William the Second
whose nickname was Rufus, 'the Red'.

Rebellion and wars, invasion by Scotland:
his kingship was bloody, it's said.

Hot-tempered and ruthless, this son of the Conqueror
was no monarch to die in his bed.

Some say he was murdered: an arrow while hunting
and Rufus the Red King bled.

Then William the Second was buried in Winchester –
curiously, minus his head.

William II
King of England, 1087 - 1100

A Heap of Henries

John Canfield

I

1100 – Henry One:
William the Conqueror's youngest son;
one brother went hunting, but came undone,
he saw his chance and made a run
for the throne, and when the deal was done,
so brother two couldn't doubt that *he'd* won
he locked him up, far away from the sun.
1135 – died with no son.

·······································

Henry I, King of England, 1100 - 1135
Henry II, King of England, 1154 - 1189
Henry III, King of England, 1216 - 1272
Henry IV, King of England, 1399 - 1413
Henry V, King of England, 1413 - 1422
Henry VI, King of England, 1422 - 1461, 1470 - 1471
Henry VII, King of England, 1485 - 1509
Henry VIII, King of England, 1509 - 1547

II

1154 – Henry Two:
Son of Empress Matilda and Geoff of Anjou,
he fought against Stephen, the King, and it's true
that they made their peace; when Steve died (boo hoo)
he took over the crown and caused quite a to do
offing Thomas à Becket, then got in a stew
with his wife when she found he had a girlfriend too.
Died 1189, out in France, *sacre bleu!*

III

1216 – Henry Three:
Became king while he was only still knee-
high, when father John got dysentery,
only nine years old, then grew up to be
a so-so ruler, quite honestly;
went to war with the barons, repeatedly,
failed to 'reclaim his lands' in Brittany,
died and was buried in Westminster Abbey.

IV

1399 – Henry Four:
Known as Bolingbroke, son of John of Gaunt,
when he died, Richard Two took his land, made him poor;
Henry put *him* in jail, bypassed Edmund de Mor-
timer, heir to the throne, from the house of York,
so the seed was sown for civil war;
spent his reign quashing rebels, such as Owain Glyndŵr.
Died in 1413; got sick, fell to the floor.

V

1413 – Henry Five:
Was the reckless Prince Hal while his dad was alive,
but when King, like an oak tree, he started to thrive:
fought the French when the odds were we'd take a nose-dive,
gave the speech of St. Crispin, to make his men strive,
so he swatted the French, like bees from a hive,
made a claim to *their* throne, took French Catherine as wife,
but then suddenly got sick and didn't survive.

VI

1422 – Henry Six:
Nine months old when dad died, and the state in a fix,
had the Hundred Years War with the French in the mix,
was their King for a while, but did not have the bricks
to build a stronger house, so the one made of sticks
came right down, and the Yorkists were up to their tricks:
Edward Four comes along with his pals, and he kicks
out the king, so, The Tower for Henry, then… nix.

VII

1485 – Henry Seven:
The first of the Tudors, defeated the felon
Richard Three at Bosworth, and then
married a York, which served to leaven
the kingdom to peace, from Scotland to Devon,
but some people weren't happy with how much was given
in taxes to Henry, the nobles were seething.
Died 1509, and perhaps went to heaven?

VIII

1509 – Henry Eight:
You'd have a great time, if you were his mate,
he liked to carouse and leave a clean plate,
and he had bold ideas about church and state,
and it is fair to say that the man liked to date,
if you made him cross, then it would seal your fate,
and in his later years he put on lots of weight.
1547 – became Henry, the late.

In the verses on Henry V and VII, John is reflecting traditional views about these kings made popular by Shakespeare. The idea that Henry V 'swatted the French' might have been shared by Shakespeare's original audience, many of whom are likely to have seen him as a conquering hero. Later actors have often made Henry a more scheming and unsavoury character.

Writing under a Tudor monarch who descended from Henry VII, it was in Shakespeare's interests to present Henry VII as a better person than Richard III, whom he defeated in battle. To this day Richard III is often viewed as a kind of pantomime villain in popular culture.

Matilda of Scotland married King Henry I in 1100. She grew up in a convent and some people believed this meant she was a nun and shouldn't be allowed to marry the king.

Matilda's Hair

Anna Kisby

Wings around her face, falling,
feathering her waist. Hair as long
as this girl is clever.

Before, she'd given hair no thought.
Too busy with her Latin, her botany,
her grammar.

Locked up here,
the Abbess declares her hair
a temptation to look upon.

Matilda of Scotland
Queen Consort of England, 1100 - 1118

Henry I
King of England, 1100 - 1135

It is woven and bound
around her head like a crown, hidden
beneath a nun's veil.

One day she will be wide-winged,
an eagle queen, wise
as she is strong.

She will be our swan – that loyal.
Song-thrush of a queen. Gentle,
keen to care.

Look now – she is clawing
the covering, the binding, from her head.
Stamping her veil underfoot.

Wings about her face, unfurling
to her waist. A banner, a flag, a jubilee –
here comes her hair.

There is a story that Matilda
told a group of bishops an
anecdote about tearing off her
veil. She was trying to prove to
them that she had never been a
nun, so was free to marry.

Matilda is traditionally known as
'Mold the Good Queen' (Mold
was another name she was known
by), for her religious commitment,
charitable works and interest in
the arts. She also helped rule the
country while Henry I was absent
and was generally considered a kind
and fair queen.

Matilda was the daughter of Henry I and Matilda of Scotland. She was married to Heinrich V, emperor and king of Germany. Matilda's son went on to become Henry II.

The Anarchy

Emma Rose Millar

Henry the First took his last regal breath,
blood-sucking eels the cause of his death.
The King kicked the bucket – his son long departed,
and that's where the mayhem and anarchy started.

Stephen
King of England, 1135 - 1154

Matilda
Holy Roman Empress, German Queen and
Queen of Italy, 1114 - 1125
Lady of the English, 1141 - 1148

Empress Matilda was the King's rightful heir,
but the chauvinist Lords cried, 'We'll never swear
our allegiance or troth to this unmanly ruler!'
and instead crowned her cousin, Stephen of Blois.

The Empress Matilda declared civil war,
there was bloodshed and carnage, chaos, uproar.
Though Stephen of Blois tried his Royal best,
mighty Matilda seized the South West.

Bedlam and brouhaha, hubbub and hassle,
the Empress besieged, inside Oxford Castle.
He thought she'd roll over and give up the feud,
but fearless Matilda could not be subdued.

One wintry evening with bright stars all blinking,
in the frail moonlight, Matilda, unflinching,
escaped from the castle – all dressed in white,
into the shadowy, snow-laden night.

The Anarchy raged on for nineteen long years,
sadness and suffering, trouble and tears,
till Stephen of Blois did what was fair,
declaring Matilda's son, Henry, his heir.

If only he'd done that back in the beginning,
instead of being dead-set on warfare and winning
against the uprising and wild anarchy
that started when Henry ate eels for his tea.

Lion Heart

Jennifer Watson

Way up high
in a sunlit sky,
a cathedral's spire stands tall,
but deep in the ground
lies a box that was found
and the ravens watch over all.

So small is that box,
with its intricate locks,
so heavy the lead of its making,
but a heavier thing
is the heart of the king
who waits for the final stock-taking.

• •

Richard I (Richard the Lionheart)
King of England, 1189 - 1199

Good King Richard,
Lion Heart!
England has burnished his story,
yet his banner unfurled
in a far distant world
with a warrior's bloodlust for glory.

Saladin's bane
but too many were slain –
the Third Crusade wasn't pretty,
and the blood of the land
seeped away in the sand
when they failed to recapture the city.

So he started for home
to reclaim England's throne
from a brother who liked the position,
but Richard bored fast,
England's lure didn't last
and he sought out some French opposition.

Then way up high
in the sunlit sky,
a crossbowman stood tall,
and his bolt flew strong
and its reach was long,
and the ravens watched over all.

And Richard knew
that his hours were few,
that the archer had done for the Lion.
So he prayed for his sins
and the price of his wins,
kissing his mum before dying.

They took him apart
and embalmed Richard's heart
with some frankincense for the aroma
and a smidgeon of mint
to give just a hint
of a king with a saintly persona.

Now way up high,
where the stone meets the sky
and the wind tugs the weathervane round,
the sun goes down
on a busy French town
and the heart of the Lion sleeps sound.

• •

Known as 'Lionheart' because
of his courage and military
aggression, Richard died in France,
where he was fighting for land.

• •

• • • • • • • • • • • • • • • •

Richard I only spent
six months of his ten-
year reign in England.

• • • • • • • • • • • • • • • •

• • • • • • • • • • • • • • • • •

This was after the Third
Crusade, where he had failed
to take Jerusalem from the
great Muslim leader, Saladin.

• • • • • • • • • • • • • • • • •

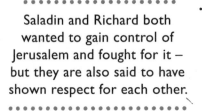

Saladin and Richard both wanted to gain control of Jerusalem and fought for it – but they are also said to have shown respect for each other.

Eventually, Saladin's armies killed so many of Richard's soldiers, and vice versa, that the two leaders agreed a three-year truce.

The Crusades lasted for hundreds of years, as European Christians fought to regain control of Jerusalem (and other places) from the Muslim rulers. It was a time of heavy bloodshed.

Many at the time saw the Crusaders as heroes, but nowadays we look much more critically at their violent invasion of a foreign country.

John, (Not Quite) King of England

Rachael M Nicholas

I've got a royal dad,
and a royal cat,
a mum who's royal
and wears a gold hat.

I've got royal hair,
and royal snot,
my teeth are royal –
the whole royal lot!

•••••••

John
King of England, 1199 - 1216

I've got a royal tongue,
and a royal head,
and when I go to sleep
it's in a royal bed.

I ride a horse
with a royal name
and every game I play
is a royal game.

I sleep royal sleep
and dream royal dreams
and my pyjamas are stitched
with gold, royal seams.

I'd be the best ever King,
I'd pass laws just for fun,
or I would, I suppose,
if I was #1 son.

See, my brother is royal,
as royal as me!
But he's further along
on our family tree.

My brother is older,
he's first and I'm not,
so I'll let him be King –
he can grab the top spot.

But I can be sneaky,
a masterful plotter,
I guess you could say
I'm a right royal rotter.

Having waited all that time to take over from his brother, Richard I, in the end John was a very unpopular king.

He was so unpopular that his barons rebelled against him and forced him to sign a document known as Magna Carta, which limited his powers and set down laws that he, the king, had to obey. This changed the nature of kingship in Britain forever.

The Song of the Spider

(inspired by the inspiring spider spied by King Robert the Bruce)

Julie Anna Douglas

I weave.
I spin.
Don't give up.
Don't give in.

When you think
failure's near.
Try again.
Face your fear.
If you slip,
get a grip.
If you stumble,
don't crumble.

I weave.
I spin.
Don't give up.
Don't give in.

Don't think
it's the end.
Turn around.
Go, my friend.
Stand up tall.
Show them all.
Leave my cave,
strong and brave.

I weave.
I spin.
Don't give up.
Don't give in.

Robert I (Robert the Bruce)
King of Scotland, 1306 - 1329

Robert the Bruce, or Robert I, was a Scottish king who fought successfully to establish Scotland's independence from England.

Centuries later, a legend emerged that exiled King Robert was hiding in a cave during his struggles against the English, when he saw a spider trying again and again to build a web.

He was inspired by the determined spider's eventual success, and went on to win the Battle of Bannockburn, even though Edward II's army was much bigger.

The official version was that Edward died of natural causes but rumours soon started circulating that he had been murdered. One very horrible story involved a red-hot poker...

King Edward II

Kate O'Neil

Why can't a king have favourites?
The favourites think it's fine.
So I had lots of favourites
until some killjoy swine

complained my habits weren't 'correct'
and had me put away.
Imagine! Locked up in a castle!
Not allowed to play.

It seems that scholars still debate
about my final minutes.
The rumour that I like the least
is *how* they fried my innards.

Edward II
King of England, 1307 - 1327

59

After the Coronation

David McKelvie

*On the day after the coronation of King
Robert III in August 1390, the Canon of a
nearby monastery came to Scone Palace:*

'I must speak to his Majesty
on a matter of some urgency,
for those coronation crowds
have trampled all our crops –
we have nothing left to gather
and the labourers want paying…
We are seeking compensation
and an audience with the King

....

Robert III
King of Scotland, 1390 - 1406

of this bold new Scottish nation
he's had the pleasure to bring in.'
And the Chamberlain said:
'Shoo, man, shoo. Away wi' yer blether!'

The second day after the coronation, the Canon returned:
'Sir, is the King now ready,
recovered from festivities
with Queens and Lords and Princes
and other such Their Majesties?
You see, those coronation crowds
have trampled every crop
and we seek a little money
to help our grumbling stop.'
And the Chamberlain said:
'Shoo, man, shoo. Away wi' yer blether!'

The third day after the coronation, the Canon returned:
'Any chance I could chat to the King?'
And the Chamberlain said:
'Shoo, man, shoo. Away wi' yer blether!'

*The fourth day after the coronation, just before sunrise, a
crowd gathered at Scone Palace – men and women, each with
a bucket and a stick – a corn doll on a pole led the parade. At
the count of three, a horn blew, rages were raised and each
stick hit each bucket. A window opened and the King glared
out. The Canon sang:*

'Dear King, dear King, we're happy
to see you here this morning
as the sun is set to rise
on this grand day dawning.
       We'll celebrate the Majesty
       by singing out a song –
       we have no work to do today
       and this August day is long.
              May we follow you all day, my Lord,
              our footsteps matching yours
              and bang our buckets, blow our horn
              as you complete your Royal Tours?'
And the King, in night gown, bleary-eyed, sighed:
'Come in, man, come in...'

This poem is based on an
incident that reportedly followed
the coronation of King Robert
III, which is recorded in Walter
Bower's epic chronicle of
Scottish history, *Scotichronicon*,
written in the 1440s.

Mo' Power, Mo' Problems or Henry IV's Lament

Meghan Ballard

It's a so-so thing
to kill a King
and to sit on his cushy throne.

You get a new house,
and perhaps a new spouse,
and can claim his Crown as your own.

But then there's the matter
of keeping the latter,
and oh, what a pain that has been.

Everyone thinks
that my policies stink:
'Henry out and _____ in!'

The number of heads
that I've cut – dead –
from rebels that sprout like weeds

· · · · · · · · · · · ·

Henry IV
King of England, 1399 - 1413

63

give my heart pause
and my conscience cause
to ask if my soul can be freed.

And I get a headache
to think on my namesake –
the boy's a bit eager, you see.

I'm not dead yet.
(Though soon I'd bet.)
But till then leave the ruling to me.

Then there's my body:
I'll admit that it's shoddy.
Cursed even, some have said.

But they should try
to live and to die
with this burden circling their head.

• • • • • • • • • • • • • • • • • •
Henry's cousin and king,
Richard II, had exiled Henry
and seized his family's lands,
following tensions between
them at court.
• • • • • • • • • • •

• •
Henry invaded England, helped
by lots of local supporters, and
Richard surrendered without a fight.
Richard was imprisoned in a castle
and died a few months later.
• •

Henry's Heart

Richard O'Brien

It's hard to be a big man when
      your dad's a big man.

It's hard to be a king at nine months old.

Sceptres scare me. Swords are worse.

They threw me on the throne
      before I learnt to write my name
(you spell it   P-L-A-N-T-A-G-A-N-E-T)

and men who said   they only wanted
  what was best for me

············

Henry VI
King of England, 1422 - 1461, 1470 - 71

took turns at power   passed me back and forth
like a human football.

You've never seen so many uncles.

When I turned sixteen,
they let me wear my own crown
    but they told me that my job was
        WAR
        and that I should get married to help sign a truce
          in the
        WAR
        but the truce didn't last and it soon only led
          to more
        WAR

and after about eight years of this
of my worries   and cares   and the noise
  of all the shouting

t h i n g s
        g o t
             a
                b i t
                     s p a c e d
                           o u t

and I didn't really know where I was
    for about a year.
        Did you hear?

Then I snapped back at Christmas to find there was still more
                WAR

not in France this time   but between my own people
and that I was   somehow   supposed
        to do something about it.

I never asked   to be asked
       to be the kind of person
who would have to do things
       about things.
                     But that's the life of kings.

And I don't quite know how
       but one day
I looked up from what must have been
       the battlefield
to find another man
       sitting on the throne
and he was very tall   which was fine by me

I could be a shepherd   I could start a library
I've started three already   can I show you?

            No.

No books.
No prayers.
No chit-chat.
Only
     WAR

until I was back on the throne
       for six frightening months,
           sitting on a spider pit.

Then the tall man was back   as if that was the way
it was always supposed to be   which as I said
    the first time   was fine by me

when I'm dead   he can be as tall as he likes

and now I am
                    and now he is.

They killed my son.
            Did I tell you that part?
                    Sometimes I forget to remember
                            a lot of what happened.

But I do know one thing:
        after I died they put my hat   next to my tomb
and you could put it on to stop yourself
                getting a headache.

Good luck to you with that is all I can say.

It never helped me at all.

In the fifteenth century, a period of fighting for the throne
broke out between two royal houses. The conflict later
became known as the Wars of the Roses, because different
colours of rose were symbols associated with each of the
Houses: white for York and red for Lancaster.

First, the House of Lancaster: this started with King Henry IV, who was succeeded by his son, Henry V and then his grandson, Henry VI.

This Henry was not as strong a leader as his father or his grandfather. He also suffered from what we today would understand as periods of mental illness.

Now, the House of York: like Henry's family, they were also descended from King Edward III. The Yorkists used the instability at court to advance their own claim to the throne.

Battles ensued between these branches of cousins for around thirty years, between 1455 and 1487.

Henry VI (Lancaster) lost the throne to Edward IV (York), then was briefly restored to power, then once again defeated in battle.

The conflict came to a close when a distant Lancastrian relative defeated York's Richard III at the Battle of Bosworth, and took power as Henry VII.

Elizabeth Woodville

Catherine Rockwood

One of these years
we'll put up our feet
and laugh till the tears
spill over our cheeks,
Jane Shore
and I.

Didn't we know
and didn't we say
how much they'd dislike it
if both of us stayed?
Jane Shore
and I.

....

Elizabeth Woodville
Queen Consort of England, 1464 - 1470, 1471 - 1483
Edward IV
King of England, 1461 - 1470, 1471 - 1483

Oh a king is a prize
bringing pageants and gold,
setting signs in the sky,
causing tales to be told
of Jane Shore
and I:

and a king is fatiguing.
He's pleased, he's forlorn;
there's a war! so he's leaving
perhaps to return
to Jane Shore
and I...

Till the day that he doesn't.
A day nothing mends.
Follow times of small comfort,
and very few friends.
But Jane Shore
and I

held ourselves steady.
We planned, and we strove:
kept all things at the ready
for allies and foes,
Jane Shore
and I.

Now the bad years are over;
my daughter's a queen.
I'm retired in Bermondsey,
Jane's married again.
Still she
and I

write to each other.
This year, or the next
she'll come over the river.
We'll meet past the Thames,
gladly,
Jane Shore
and I.

Elizabeth Woodville was the wife
of Edward IV and Jane Shore was
one of his mistresses (someone he
was having a relationship with at
the same time as having a wife).

After Edward IV's death, Elizabeth was accused of plotting with Jane Shore against the late king's brother (the future Richard III), though historians are not sure this plot really happened.

Elizabeth's daughter, Elizabeth of York, married Henry Tudor, who defeated Richard III at the Battle of Bosworth Field and became King Henry VII.

This battle and this marriage (which brought the competing sides together) ended the Wars of the Roses.

Edward V

Mary Anne Clark

Oh stop – and let me catch your hand –
I'll speak so briefly. Will you hear?

I don't want money – understand
that like a day-dream I appear

in flashes, gone. You wouldn't sneer
if you knew me. The wind is cold
to one like me, so young, so old.

Edward V
King of England, 9th April 1483 - 25th June 1483

73

I'll speak fast. I'd have loved to stand
before my murmuring court, assessing

right and wrong; waving my hand
to summon sudden quiet; processing

in state to mount my throne; addressing
ambassadors – one word from me
sending peace or war across the sea.

But you won't find that in history.
I was a boy and men drew up

a plan to hush me. Mystery?
I'm Edward, king who never grew up,

and long ago the ground threw up
my memory. I'm lost boy, freak
of time, and only echoes speak.

• •

Richard made a case for why
Edward V could not be the
legitimate heir of Edward IV
and Parliament agreed.

• • • • • • • • • • • • • • • • • •

• •

Soon after, Edward and his younger
brother disappeared from the Tower of
London. The cause of their death is one
of English history's big mysteries.

• •

King of the Car Park

Elli Woollard

The body of Richard III was recently discovered under a car park in Leicester.

I'm the King of the Car Park.
Trucks trundle over my bones.
I'm the King of the Car Park.
My body is buried in stones.
I'm the King of the Car Park.
Surrounded by gaseous fumes.
I'm the King of the Car Park.
Nobody gave me a tomb.
I'm the King of the Car Park.

....

Richard III
King of England, 1483 - 1485

Scooters skid over my skull.
I'm the King of the Car Park
and life here is... well, rather dull.
I'm the King of the Car Park.
I'll never again see my castle.
But still I'm a king, and that's the thing,
so you're the dirty rascal!

Historians disagree about what
Richard III was like. Most scholars
think it is likely that his nephews,
the Princes in the Tower, were
killed on Richard's orders.

But was he the evil murderer of
Shakespeare's play, or more an
uninspiring king who couldn't
prevent unrest and rebellion?

Richard's unearthed skeleton showed
that he had scoliosis – a curved spine
– but there was no sign of the limp
and withered arm of Shakespearean
legend and the popular imagination.
Richard was reburied in Leicester
Cathedral in 2015.

Lambert Simnel

Catherine Rockwood

Some are born to greatness
and some to play the fool.
I can manage both, dear!
I'm the good King of Misrule.

From fair Dublin to Furness,
Furness to Roecliffe Moor,
my troops are trooping south, dear,
and we'll visit you for sure.

. . . .

Lambert Simnel
Pretender, crowned in 1487

We've drums and noise aplenty
and banners with triple crowns
that make your old king edgy.
Come join us! Bring your town!

If the Earl of Oxford rages,
grinding his stony teeth,
tell him it's all in fun, dear,
and fun cannot be beat.

No he can't beat laughter from us
or the warmth of a summer's day
as we travel cheerfully on, dear,
well prepared to play.

We're all prepared to play, now,
in our hauberks and brigandines,
with our *swerdys*, *speris* and *gonnes*, dear –
all primed and polished clean.

Come join us, step along lightly!
Consider, this isn't a fight.
It's a jest that can go wrong or rightly,
a fist that can tickle or smite.

King Henry is putting his gloves on,
he's riding to meet us now
with his *haubergeons*, *gonnes* and *bowes*
and dear, you must stay for the show.

King Henry VII's enemies decided to pretend that Lambert Simnel was a descendant of the Yorkist King Edward IV. They claimed that he had escaped from the Tower of London and was the real heir to the throne.

In fact, Lambert was simply the young son of a craftsman from Oxford (probably), but he got swept up in a plot that took him to Dublin, Ireland, where he was crowned as 'Edward VI', then on to the bloody Battle of Stoke.

Here he was captured, though Henry forgave him and gave him a job as a kitchen servant and then a falconer!

'Hauberks' and 'brigandines' are types of armour. 'Swerdys, speris and gonnes' are old-fashioned spellings for swords, spears and guns.

79

Henry VII's marmoset

Kate Wise

If one more minion calls me Monkey,
I think I'm going to scream.
Or throw something at them. Hard.
I know, it doesn't seem
like I should be ungrateful.
I know; I have everything I need.
I've got pearls and lace in a ruff round my face
and a dog to be my pony.
Henry's taught me to make rude gestures
he thinks I don't really understand

....

Henry VII
King of England, 1485 - 1509

There is a story, recorded by
Francis Bacon in his history of
Henry VII's reign, that the king
had a pet monkey which tore up
the notebook where Henry kept
his 'pensive accounts', secretive
observations about people
around him.

A minion is a follower
of a powerful leader
– especially quite a
lowly servant.

but I'm just plotting my next move,
and these tiny hairy hands
are powerful. Believe me.
See his little notebook there?
Full of suspicions, conspiracy!
Just imagine if, say, I tore it up –
how much lost History?!
You can keep your food on silver,
your flounces and finery.
I'd rather run wild in the countryside
and the truth is – so would he.

Queen of Hearts

Anna Kisby

Elizabeth of York enjoyed a flutter: rolling dice, shuffling packs, she gambled left, right, centre. But on, the Henrys (7 &8) how they loved her! Skin of white roses, red-gold hair, scent of bread & honey. We honour her full heart and her (the grandmother of Good Queen Bess) with her stiff headdress. Her picture on your playing card.

Some believe that the Queen of Hearts, in a pack of playing cards, was modelled on Elizabeth of York.

Elizabeth of York
Queen Consort of England, 1486 - 1503

Henry VII
King of England, 1485 - 1509

The Six Wives

Carole Bromley

King Henry VIII wanted a son
but none of his wives could give him one
so he got rid of them, one by one.

Katherine of Aragon was first to go:
he went to the Pope and the Pope said no
but Henry was a stubborn so and so.

Divorced her anyway, for Anne Boleyn,
but she was too flirtatious for him
so Henry gave her neck a trim.

· · · · · · · · · · · · · ·

Henry VIII
King of England, 1509 - 1547

83

Jane Seymour next and here's a thing:
the very next day she was wearing his ring
but she'd only live for one more spring

so Anne of Cleves was then lined up
but the king didn't find her cute enough
and he ordered his men to buy her off.

Then Catherine Howard. Lasted a year
and when she didn't produce an heir
the executioner took her by the hair.

Katherine Parr was chosen instead,
twenty years younger, quiet, well-bred,
smart enough to keep her head.

Katherine of Aragon
Queen Consort of England, 1509 - 1533

Anne Boleyn
Queen Consort of England, 1533 - 1536

Jane Seymour
Queen Consort of England, 1536 - 1537

Anne of Cleves
Queen Consort of England, January 1540 - July 1540

Catherine Howard
Queen Consort of England, 1540 - 1541

Katherine Parr
Queen Consort of England, 1543 - 1547

The Importance of Keeping One's Head

Shauna Darling Robertson

Oh Mother dear, squawked Anne Boleyn,
I don't know what to do.
King Henry's asked for fowl tonight
but all I have is stew.
You've got to keep your head, said Ma,
for flapping will not do.
You're right, said Anne and trundled down
to Tesco at the edge of town
and bought a ready-roast for two.
Divine! said Henry. Well done you!

Oh Father dear, the good queen wailed,
I'm up to here with stress.
King Henry wants me on trombone
but all I play is chess.
You've got to keep your head my girl,
said Pa, and lose it less.
Good move, said Anne and without fuss

. . . .

Henry VIII
King of England, 1509 - 1547

Anne Boleyn
Queen Consort of England, 1533 - 1536

clicked 'buy now' at Trombones-R-Us
and typed in her address.
Well blow me down! said Henry, I'm impressed!

Oh Doctor dear, the queen despaired,
prescribe me parenthood.
King Henry wants a son and heir
but so far, not so good.
You've got to keep your head, urged Doc,
if I were you, I would…
A fruitful view, the queen agreed
while Henry passed his grave decree:
My queen, she must bear better!
I will, begged Anne, I'll keep my head.
But Henry didn't let her.

Monarchs throughout history have often
been unpredictable and demanding. Anne
knew the pressure was on her to have a
baby boy, and Henry unfairly blamed her
for not producing a male heir.

Eventually Henry turned against his wife
and started to listen to her enemies, who
claimed that she had been unfaithful. She
was beheaded in public, the first English
queen to suffer this fate.

· · · · · · · · · · · · · · · · · · · ·
There is a popular belief
that Henry VIII wrote the
song 'Greensleeves', though
most historians don't think
this is true.
· · · · · · · · ·

· · · · · · · · · · · · · · · · · · ·
The head of the Catholic
Church, whom Henry
defied in divorcing his
first wife, was the Pope
in Rome.
· · · · · · · ·

Henry VIII

Rachel Piercey

To the tune of 'Greensleeves'

Seven Henries ruled before:
I was the Eighth, I was the last.
I liked to dance and go to war,
I liked to marry, read and joust.

Husband, soldier, killer, king.
Can I control what the world believes?
I did do many significant things,
but I probably didn't write Greensleeves.

I did build up the Royal Navy,
I did break with the Church of Rome,
I did eat lots of Tudor gravy,
I didn't like to be alone.

· · · · · · · · · · · ·
Henry VIII
King of England, 1509 - 1547

I did have three best friends called Tom
but we're no longer thick as thieves...
I did get cruel when things went wrong,
but I probably didn't write Greensleeves.

My spending did get out of hand.
I did destroy the monasteries.
I did send actors round the land
to spread word of my majesty.

I went through wives till I got old
(one of my many royal peeves –
like France and Scotland, gout, no gold)
but I probably didn't write Greensleeves.

Did I regret what I had done?
And did my heart break many times?
And did I miss my friends long-gone?
And can a king commit a crime?

You can't be sure that history
knows everything a king achieves.
I had a busy monarchy
but I probably didn't write Greensleeves.

Thomas More, Thomas
Cromwell and Thomas
Cranmer all worked for
the king. Advising Henry
and carrying out his
orders was not easy.

Henry eventually had
More and Cromwell
executed for treason.

'Kat' in the first
verse refers to
Katherine Astley,
who was Elizabeth's
governess.

Dear Kate

Catherine Olver

Letters from the young Elizabeth I to Queen Katherine Parr

Dear Queen Katherine, *12th July 1543*
Congratulations on becoming Daddy's sixth wife.
I pray he lets you live a long and happy life.
Kat says you're kind and sensible, as well as pretty,
so please don't be a traitor too. That would be a pity.
Polite Regards, the Lady Elizabeth (age 9)

. . . .

Elizabeth I
Queen of England, 1558 - 1603
Katherine Parr
Queen Consort of England, 1543 - 1547

89

Dear Queen Kate, *7th September 1544*
I know you're busy (ruling England)
while Dad's at war in France
but would you come and watch me
in my first court dance?
     Love from, Elizabeth (11 today!)

Dear Queen Kate, *1st January 1545*
Happy fifteen-forty-five. In celebration,
here's a French prayerbook with my own translation.
Mary says she's not sure who's the snottiest geek,
Edward or me. In truth, I'm better at Greek.
(I don't intend to boast and I'm not supposed to know this
but Master Grindal thinks I've made impressive progress.)
I made the bookmark too. It took me ages to embroider.
     with love, Elizabeth
p.s. Please could *you* ask Mary why she's always cross with me?
We meet in corridors; curtseying, I stand aside
but she glares at me so hurtfully I've started to hide
behind the nearest tapestry in order to avoid her.

Dear Kate, *13th March 1546*
I know you're busy because Dad has gout
but I'm having a crisis of religious doubt
and I don't know who else to talk to.
     in secrecy, Elizabeth

Dear Kate, *3rd February 1547*
Thank you – more than any words – for letting me stay
and live with you, happily free and away

from the labyrinthine politics of Edward's court.
There's no place like Chelsea for quiet thought:
I'll sit by the oak in the heart of the maze,
just thinking, for days…
   with love, Elizabeth

  Dear Kate, *9th June 1548*
Your book of *Lamentation* feels so heavy in my hands
even my steps are burdened – which were yesterday so light,
galloping the Galliard, turning the Tourdion with Thom,
echoing Jane's down the chapel to say our psalms,
or keeping up with you, Kate, in dancing and in prayer.
I can picture your serious stare, your lips moving as you wrote it,
but the book in my hands is a lonely replacement
for walking arm-in-arm with you through the rose garden,
reading instead your mock-serious mouth and delighted eyes
the moment you spot Thom's lordly loitering in the hedge
and pretend surprise. I wish I were there,
with you, with Thom, with Jane,
but wherever I go – wherever I'm sent – I remain
   your loving Elizabeth

  Dear Kate, *2nd September 1548*
Congratulations on the birth! I wanted to come
but Thom said you were too weak to visit.
You survived Dad – childbirth's not so bad, is it?
Please don't die without saying goodbye.
You're the closest thing I ever had to a mum.
   Your loving daughter, Elizabeth

When their half-brother Edward was born, Henry VIII took Mary and Elizabeth off the list of family who could inherit the throne. Katherine Parr helped persuade Henry to put them back in line for the throne. So, without Katherine, Elizabeth might never have become queen!

Katherine was also the first woman in England to publish a book in English under her own name, rather than anonymously. Her best-known book, *The Lamentation of a Sinner*, was published in 1547.

After Henry VIII's death, Elizabeth lived in Katherine's household (as did Lady Jane Grey, the subject of the next poem), but she was sent away when Katherine's new husband, Thomas Seymour, started paying her too much attention.

Katherine gave birth to a daughter, Mary Seymour, but died of infection in September 1548, just before Elizabeth's 15th birthday.

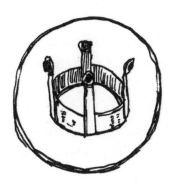

July, Jane

Rachael M Nicholas

Nine days in July.
That's all.
That's it.
A small cup of time.
Not long enough for the news
to stop being new.
I can count it all up on my fingers
and still have one left over
to keep me company.

· · · · · · · · · · · · · · · · · · ·

Lady Jane Grey
Queen of England, 10th July 1553 - 19th July 1553

Nine days in July.
Were they warm?
Did I stop for a minute
in a garden and feel the soft, honey
sun on my face?
And the birds. Did I name
the birds I saw from my window?
Each one its own separate self,
just like me.

Nine days in July.
Exciting and frightening.
Blurry and brief. I was brave.
I waited for England.
I slept in a strange room and thought
about all the strange rooms to come
and the strangers in them,
their eyes,
and what they might say.

Nine days in July.
You are never just one thing,
but I was always Jane.
When I woke up I was Jane,
and when I went to sleep,
and when I was Queen,
and then when I wasn't again.
I was Jane when it started,
and Jane at the end, when it ended.

The question of who would inherit the throne after a monarch died was often very complicated. In 16th century England, religion played a big part in this, because of Henry VIII's divorce.

When the Catholic Church wouldn't allow Henry to get divorced from Katherine of Aragon, he responded by leaving the Church and making England a Protestant country instead.

When Edward VI was dying in 1553, he really didn't want his half-sister Mary to become Queen, because she was a Catholic. He was persuaded by his advisers to promise the crown to his cousin Jane Grey, who held strongly Protestant beliefs.

Reports suggest that Jane didn't even want the crown. Unfortunately for her, the Catholic Mary had powerful friends and was soon able to remove her from the throne. She was accused of treason, and executed at the age of just sixteen.

A short rhyme
for a short reign:
Lady Jane Grey

Jerrold Bowam

God save Jane,
long may she reign

or for nine days until
another's will

wins priority.
God save Mary.

· · · · · · · · · · · · · · · · · ·

Lady Jane Grey
Queen of England, 10th July 1553 - 19th July 1553

Bloody Mary

Melanie Branton

Mary the First, or Mary Tudor,
acquired a nickname somewhat ruder:
because she was so cruel and scary,
the people called her Bloody Mary.

They called her that because, indeed,
she made a lot of people bleed.
She bled you, buddy, till you bled;
her bloody hands were bloody red.

·······························

Mary I (Bloody Mary)
Queen of England, 1553 - 1558
Queen Consort of Spain, 1556 - 1558

You had to do just what she said
and not do what you want, instead,
as things could soon get ruddy hairy
with fuddy duddy Bloody Mary.

For Bloody Mary, Mary Tudor,
no matter from which side you viewed her,
was, shall we say, perhaps a smidgen
OTT about religion?

In fact, it made her feel quite sick
to hear you weren't a Catholic.
She wouldn't hesitate a minute
to build a fire and put you in it.

For lunch, whatever time that this be,
she'd roast you till your skin was crispy
or send you on your way to heaven
by baking you at Gas Mark 7.

She filled her subjects' hearts with dread
and those who crossed her wound up dead,
and everyone was very wary
of scary, lairy, Bloody Mary.

The official religion of England changed several times during the sixteenth century. Catholics and Protestants were both branches of the Christian religion, but had different views on a range of subjects. Believers in the two faiths also became political opponents.

Mary was a Catholic like her mother, Katherine of Aragon. When she took power, she made England a Catholic country once more.

She appointed as her Archbishop of Canterbury Reginald Pole, who believed that heretics (ie people who didn't share their version of religion) should be executed to set an example.

Under Mary's reign, many believers in the Protestant faith were arrested and burnt at the stake.

Love Letter from Mary Tudor to her Husband Philip of Spain

Brian Moses

Dear Philip, my Phil
  it's making me ill
to think that
  you don't love me.
I love you my dear
  but you're making it clear
that this marriage
  was not meant to be.

I'm here all alone,
  if only you'd phone,
send a pigeon
  or simply just write.
Invite me, please do,
  Ibiza with you
would soon set
  our marriage alight.

Dear Philip, my love,
  my sweet turtle dove,
I know it's with you
  I relate.
I wish you'd return
  and help me to burn
all those plotting
  against the state.

Everybody I know
  says you should go,
but I need you
  to give me an heir.
Do you think that I'm neater
  than a sweet senorita
or do your eyes
  wander elsewhere?

Mary I (Bloody Mary)
Queen of England, 1553 - 1558
Queen Consort of Spain, 1556 - 1558

Philip II
King of Spain, 1556 - 1598
King of Portugal & the Algarves, 1581 - 1598
King of England, 1554 - 1558

When Queen Mary chose Philip, the heir to the throne of Spain, for her husband, many people in England were unhappy.

They were worried that having a foreign ruler married to their Queen would mean another country had power and influence over England.

Dear Philip, I'm willing
   to share double billing,
if our love could be
   reignited.
Then our reign as one
   will be equal to none,
King and Queen of
   two countries united.

They especially didn't want Philip to become King of England in his own right if Mary died, and people in Parliament wrote a complicated treaty to stop that happening.

So Philip, my Phil,
   come home, say you will,
without you it's really
   quite scary.
Forsake sunny Spain
   for the cold English rain
and the arms of
   your loving wife, Mary.

Many people also didn't want English troops getting involved in the religious wars which were ongoing in Europe.

Philip was, however, quite keen on the religious wars ongoing in Europe, and eventually joined the fray in France in 1557, which meant he was often away.

Elizabeth I's
Art of War

Kirsten Irving

See but say nothing.
Look forward and back.
Learn to chat in Irish,
Welsh and Scots.
Don't bother with husbands
or children. Don't tell
anybody of course. Let them
come, let them court you. Don't
let them short-change you

• • • • • • • • • • • • • •

Elizabeth I
Queen of England, 1558 - 1603

or elbow you out on the way
to your throne.
Stay civil, be graceful,
and keep your head on.
Send armies like locusts,
take ships,
take out leaders.
Drop warnings, not tears.
Sport pearl-drop earrings.
If your bolshy cousin
gets too much power,
remove her roughly to a tower.
Be red. Be watchful.
Trust your own mind.
Wear a big ruff. The biggest
white ruff you can find.

. . . .

Elizabeth I is one of the most
famous monarchs in history.
She was highly educated and
intelligent and, as Kirsten
explores here, her image was
something she crafted carefully.

. . . .

. . . .

She was keenly aware that
there were many groups of
advisers around her jockeying
for power and influence.
Any marriage she chose for
herself would have political
consequences – and so she
never married at all.

. . . .

Beheaded

Aileen Ballantyne

Maidservant to Mary, Queen of Scots:
Fotheringhay Castle, February, 1587:

'They pulled ye doon tae yer knees, lady,
an took aff yer kirtle tae shew that they cuid,
left yir white throat shilpit-bare.

In manus tuas, Domine, ma lady,
in manus tuas Domine, ma lady.

Ye kivered the white o yer hair,
yer hair that was yince rosey-licht –
white hair sae young in a lass.

In manus tuas, Domine, ma lady,
in manus tuas Domine, ma lady.

They spaittered the Skye terrier dug,
that hid in yer skirts, wi yer bluid.
An ah held the white lace in ma haun.

In manus tuas, Domine, ma lady,
in manus tuas Domine, ma lady.

Ah haud it, still warm, in ma palm,
bone-lace wreathed wi the scent o yer skin,
an ah'll say it for ye, ma lady:

In manus tuas Domine, ma lady,
in manus tuas Domine.'

Elizabeth I's councillors wanted her to give birth to a (Protestant) heir. When it became clear this wasn't going to happen, people started to fear that the crown might pass to Mary, Queen of Scots, Elizabeth's Catholic cousin.

In 1567, Mary gave up the Scottish throne and fled to England to seek shelter. Instead, she ended up being kept prisoner for nearly twenty years.

There were a lot of Catholic plots against the Queen during this time, and Elizabeth's advisers accused Mary of being involved in one such plot in 1586. This accusation led to her execution.

'In manus tuas Domine' means 'Into the Hands of the Lord'. It was part of the Latin prayer said by Mary, Queen of Scots, just before she was beheaded. Mary was not allowed to have a Catholic priest present when she died.

Glossary

shilpit – painfully thin
kivered – covered
yince – once
spaittered – spattered
dug – dog
bluid – blood
haun – hand

Mary, Queen of Scots (Mary Stuart)
Queen of Scotland, 1542 - 1567
Queen Consort of France, 1559 - 1560

Now That I'm Headless

Suzanne Olivante

*The ghost of Mary, Queen of Scots, is said
to haunt many Scottish castles...*

Ghostly and guiltless
My spirit restless
Can't wear a necklace
Now that I'm headless
I couldn't care less
Wish you would stare less
Standing so nervous
Startled and speechless
Did you just witness
Ghost in a pink dress
Hoping to impress
Faded and bloodless
Back from my deadness
With rigor mortis
Trailing the coldness
Drifting and wordless
Sliding my stiffness
Over the surface
Hovering helpless

Suffering sadness
Feel like an actress
Haughty in grandness
Royal but ruleless
My smile is rictus
Touch my translucence
Vaporous mistress
Ghost life is timeless
Play hocus pocus
Though never homeless
I feel aloneness
Mourning but tearless
Scotland is Queenless

Faithful and famous
My spirit restless
Can't wear a necklace
Now that I'm headless

Mary, Queen of Scots (Mary Stuart)
Queen of Scotland, 1542 - 1567
Queen Consort of France, 1559 - 1560

When Elizabeth I was
dying, she finally named
an heir: King James VI
of Scotland, the son of
Mary, Queen of Scots.

Unlike his mother,
he was raised as a
Protestant. On becoming
James I of England, he
soon encountered a
Catholic plot against him.

Gunpowder

Emma Rose Millar

With mighty Queen Bess not cold in the ground,
King James rushed to London to snatch up her crown,
for the Queen had no children – her siblings were dead,
so the monarchy rested on James Stuart's head.

James I of England and VI of Scotland
King of Scotland, 1567 - 1625
King of England, 1603 - 1625

Now James had ruled Scotland since he was a tot,
and his guardians all had been poisoned or shot,
his father was slain and his mother beheaded…
the King in his torment grew fearful and fretted.

He was anxious, distrustful, tense and suspicious,
believing that witches, corrupt and malicious,
were working against him to scupper his health,
to bring plague and famine and steal Royal wealth.

Indeed, James accused over three hundred women
of devilry, magic and trying to kill him.
But all these dark thoughts and his ghoulish obsessions
with seeking out witches and forcing confessions,

meant he could not see his villainous foes
hatching their wicked plan under his nose.
The scoundrel Guy Fawkes and his treacherous team
had cunning and wit and an audacious scheme,

ready and willing to light the touch paper
of their cunning, explosive and murderous caper,
to blow up the Lords, to cause a great blast,
with barrels of gunpowder they had amassed.

One massive *BANG!* and King James would be dead,
his Catholic daughter crowned monarch instead.
But the plot was revealed anonymously
to officials, who of course consequently

conducted a search and found Guy Fawkes untrembling,
with the barrels of gunpowder he'd been assembling.
Guy Fawkes and his seven dishonourable friends
were hung, drawn and quartered – but that wasn't the end,

for every year, on the fifth of November,
we light fireworks so we can remember
Guy Fawkes and his fiendish, nefarious ring,
who tried and then failed to blow up the King.

Guy Fawkes was not, in fact,
the mastermind of this plot -
but being found in the cellars
of the Houses of Parliament
with thirty-six barrels of
gunpowder and a 9-inch match,
it must have been hard for him
to think of a good excuse.

Later in life, James
commissioned a new
translation of the Bible into
English. The King James Version
of the Bible, finished in 1611, is
still used today in churches all
around the world.

Queen Anne's Lace

Fiona Mills

Frothy heads of soft white blooms
dance in the countryside,
remind us of the child queen
who was King James's bride.

Lowered head of golden hair,
deft fingers, fast as light,
young Queen Anne is making lace
like flowers, pure and white.

Courtly ladies bow their heads,
watching their queen so fair,
but no matter how they try,
their lacework can't compare.

Queen Anne holds her head up high,
a smile upon her face,
and cow parsley, to this day,
is known as Queen Anne's lace.

Queen Anne's Lace is a prettier name for cow parsley. There are lots of stories behind the name, but Fiona's favourite one is that when the fourteen-year-old Danish princess Anne arrived as Queen of Scotland, her handiwork so impressed the ladies at court that they named the hedgerow flower after her. Only she, it was said, could make lace as fine as those delicate blooms.

Anne of Denmark
Queen Consort of Scotland and England, 1603 - 1619
James I of England and VI of Scotland
King of Scotland, 1567 - 1625
King of England, 1603 - 1625

Interregnum
(1649-1660)

Laura Mucha

The king's head topples,
discarded rotten cabbage:
who is in charge now?

• •

In 1642, a Civil War broke out in
England. Historians have different
views on what exactly led to the
outbreak of war, but Charles
I (James's son) had become
widely unpopular for his reckless
spending, his religious views, and
his unwillingness to listen to the
demands of Parliament.

• • • • • • • • • • • • • • • •

The resulting conflict ended in
1649, when Charles I was tried
for treason and executed. For
eleven years, the country was
ruled as a republic, with no
monarch. Instead, one of the
rebels' commanders, Oliver
Cromwell, was in charge of the
new government.

• • • • • • • • • • • • •

Commonwealth of England
Republic / no monarch: 1649 - 1660

Grandad Oak and Charles II

Ros Woolner

I may be just a little tree,
no taller than a tall man's knee,
but all day long my branches sing:
My grandad, my grandad saved a king.

Back then, in sixteen fifty-one,
a future king was on the run.
Now underground my deep roots sing:
My grandad, my grandad saved a king.

....

Charles II
King of England & Scotland, 1660 - 1685
King of Scotland, 1649 - 1651

Charles climbed an oak at Boscobel,
which sheltered him and hid him well.
And all night long my young leaves sing:
My grandad, my grandad saved a king.

Though Cromwell's men were everywhere,
they didn't think to look up there.
That's why my thousand acorns sing:
My grandad, my grandad saved a king.

When, nine years later, Charles was crowned,
that oak was known for miles around.
So, woods and forests, hear me sing:
My grandad, my grandad saved a king.

Having deposed King Charles I,
Oliver Cromwell nominated his
own son to succeed him when
he died – just like the king might
have done before him! But Richard
Cromwell didn't inspire much
confidence as a ruler.

Charles, the son of the executed
king, had escaped the war against
his father – he really did hide in
an oak tree, near Worcester. He
then made his way to the coast
disguised as a servant and went to
live in exile in Europe.

Military commanders invited
Charles II back to England, if he
agreed to respect the role of
Parliament in ruling the country.
Charles returned from Europe and
to his father's throne: this event
was known as the Restoration.

In 1662, King Charles II married
Portuguese Princess Catherine of
Braganza, who popularised tea-
drinking in England.

Tea plantations have long been
associated with appalling working
conditions, and the fashion for adding
sugar to tea helped sustain the
sugar plantations of America and the
Caribbean, which used slave labour.

Anna's poem shows how,
beneath the 'official' version
of royal history, there is often
oppression and suffering.

A Nice Cup of Tea and a Sit Down

Anna Kisby

From the bottom of our hearts
we thank you Catherine of Braganza
for marrying our King Charles!
For stirring our history with flavour
by crossing the sea and gifting us tea
we toast you with this cuppa!

*

From the dregs of our cups
we remember Catherine of Braganza
who married dandy King Charles!
Who stirred up our taste
for tea-drinking days so our history is bitter
with plantations of slaves!

....

Charles II
King of England & Scotland, 1660 - 1685
King of Scotland, 1649 - 1651

Catherine of Braganza
Queen Consort of England & Scotland, 1662 - 1685

Dear William of Orange

Richard O'Brien

1.

We are the English Protestants,
and we declare (it's not a stunt)
that Catholics aren't fit to wear the crown.
That Roman rot has worn us down –
the gaudy gold, the smoky scent,
the fact they keep dissolving Parliament
like sugar in a cup of tea

∙∙∙

William III (William of Orange)
King of England & Scotland, 1689 - 1702
Stadtholder of Holland, Zeeland, Utrecht,
Gelderland and Overijssel, 1672 - 1702
Prince of Orange, 1650 - 1702

Mary II
Queen of England & Scotland, 1689 - 1694

so they don't have to hear the people's pleas...
no, we're afraid it's really *not* our thing.
And so we're asking: will you be our King?

2.

We really mean it; we're not playing games.
He's full of popery, our monarch, James
the Second. Second? He should be the last!
We've headed off bad monarchs in the past...
Forget that part. But this is out of hand –
his heir's a Catholic prince, and that won't stand.
So bring your fighting men and fighting ships –
we'll hold a feast to greet you. Fish and chips?
Oh, but perhaps that's not your style: you're Dutch.
Waffles! Fried tulips! Nothing is too much!!!

3.

Billy, we're baffled. Did you get our letters?
You can't have had an offer any better!
You needn't lift a finger to invade us
we're giving you our country on a plate, boss!
Your ships can dock at Plymouth, or Torbay.
The journey's easy. Could you come today?!
No pressure. We just really need a sovereign
who shares our faith in... God, why are we bothering?
Let's just be a republic. Can't be harder
than – you'll come? God save the King! Your Highness!
                              Quick, boys – to the harbour!

James II was a Catholic. When he came to the throne after his brother Charles's death, he tried to pressure Parliament into passing laws which made life easier for other Catholics.

At the time, this idea of religious tolerance was hugely unpopular. Forty years after the Civil War, English law-makers were *very* suspicious of a king trying to overturn their power.

When James II had a son, there was a Catholic heir to the English throne: this was the last straw. But James's daughter Mary was married to a powerful Protestant ruler – the Dutch prince William of Orange.

So William was invited to England by members of Parliament who opposed James, because they wanted him to intervene in the situation.

Defeated in battle, James II fled to France. Parliament eventually offered William the crown instead – but only if he would agree to certain limits on his rule.

This is considered another step towards 'constitutional monarchy' – a system which means the king or queen doesn't have absolute power. William and Mary were then declared the new joint rulers of England, Scotland and Ireland.

The Ballad of William III

John Canfield

Come gather round to hear the tale
of William of Orange,
the Prince from Holland, who set sail –
but wait, what rhymes with Orange?

He and wife Mary came across
to claim the regal purple,
to jointly rule as England's boss
so they could... hang on, purple?

....

William III (William of Orange)
King of England & Scotland, 1689 - 1702
Stadtholder of Holland, Zeeland, Utrecht,
Gelderland and Overijssel, 1672 - 1702
Prince of Orange, 1650 - 1702

Mary and Bill put crowns on heads
back in the eighty-ninth
year of the grand sixteen hundreds –
oh yikes, what rhymes with ninth?

They jointly ruled, till Mary died
and Bill was a lone wolf.
A king with no queen by his side:
he felt ever so... dolf?

He helped set up a national bank
which made coins out of silver,
and put his face on them, no blank
cheque. Argh! What rhymes with silver?

It's said that many people knew
King Billy liked a pint
of ale, but still, guess what? It's true
that no word rhymes with pint.

King Billy caught a chill and died,
in March, that was the month.
They buried him next to his bride
and, oh, I give up – month.

So, that was William the Third,
known as William of Orange,
who sadly never made up words
like blurple, bonth or borange.

The Bank of England, created by William, still exists today. One of the main reasons for its creation was to fund a costly war with France. This continued a centuries-old tradition of kings asking Parliament to help them find money for costly wars with France!

Supporters of the deposed King James were called Jacobites. Though William actually died of a fever, soon before this he was injured when his horse stumbled on a molehill, throwing the king to the ground.

His Jacobite opponents were delighted with this fact, and for years later would toast the mole as a supporter of their cause: 'the little gentleman in black velvet'.

William and Mary did not have any children, and so Mary's sister Anne was their heir.

Queen Anne

Rachel Piercey

There aren't too many fans
of Queen Anne.

Ex-BFF Sarah wrote a book
bad-mouthing her brain and her looks

and it went down in history.
Biography by frenemy!

Look, I'm not saying the queen
was never selfish or mean,

because she could be.
She also knew her share of tragedy.

I guess I'm just saying, let's be fairer,
and not rely on Sarah.

· · · · · · · ·

Anne
Queen of England & Scotland, 1702 - 1707
Queen of Great Britain, 1707 - 1714

Sarah in the poem is Sarah Churchill, Duchess of Marlborough. She was once a great favourite of Queen Anne's, but they fell out over politics, grief, Sarah's long absences and a clash of personalities.

In 1707, Anne's Parliament passed the Act of Union: a legal document which created a new nation, Great Britain, by combining England and Scotland ('England' at the time was considered to include Wales).

Both countries had had the same ruler for a long time, starting with James I of England who was already James VI of Scotland when he took the throne. Now they also shared one integrated Parliament.

Because none of Anne's children survived into adulthood, she had no direct heirs. There were members of the royal family who could inherit the throne, but from Parliament's view there was a problem (and by now you probably know where this is going...) – they were all Catholics!

Parliament therefore passed an Act of Settlement in 1701 which promised the throne to Anne's nearest Protestant relative. This was another descendant of James I: Sophia of Hanover, in what's now Germany.

There were more than fifty Catholics more closely related to Anne than Sophia, but this law meant she could leapfrog them all! When Sophia died two months before Anne, her son George became the next heir to the British throne.

Pushing in

Ros Woolner

If there's a queue
the whole world knows
you wait your turn.
That's how it goes.

There was a queue
in Queen Anne's time.
There always is –
it's called a line.

The first in line
(and number two)
were Catholics.
What did Anne do?

She skipped them both
(and several more),
picked George the First
and changed the law.

So, though it's true
you don't push in,
George could, and did.
They made him king.

George I
King of Great Britain, 1714 - 1727
Elector of Hanover, 1698 - 1727

King George III Observes the Transit of Venus in Richmond on June 3rd, 1769

Richard O'Brien

When George looks down the royal telescope
he's had commissioned, he can see *himself*
aged ten, performing in a play;
aged eighty, with a harpsichord,
his eyes two marbles, white
as Weymouth sea-foam;
signing a note
that says he'll stop
being
the king;
a doctor's cup;
a buckled coat;
quiet card games at home;
music by candlelight;
his grandfather lifting a sword,
inspecting military parades;
a blur across the Sun. 'To our good health!'
the King toasts the astronomer, and hopes.

....

George III
King of Great Britain, 1760 - 1820
Elector of Hanover, 1760 - 1820

125

George III was the grandson of George I, who 'pushed in' in the last poem. He lived a long life, but much of it was disrupted by periods of what we'd now think of as mental illness.

Doctors at the time dealt with these episodes in ways which today we would consider as cruel and ineffective. Like Henry VI earlier in the book, it was hard for him to rule the country while experiencing these symptoms.

So, in practice, his son (another George!) took over running the country, without actually becoming king: this way of passing power from the monarch to another person is called a regency.

George III had a lot of hobbies and interests, many of which are mentioned in Richard's poem. He was a keen amateur astronomer, and made observations of events in the night sky.

George IV's marriage with Caroline had been unhappy from the very beginning. On meeting her future husband, she remarked that he was 'nothing like as handsome as his portrait'. The prince was neglectful and unfaithful, and he accused his wife of the same thing.

126

My Favourite Queen

Toby Sligo

Out of all the kings and queens
in history,
my favourite has to be
Queen Caroline.

'Why is that, Toby?'
I hear you ask.

Well, I'll tell you.

It's because Queen Caroline
is the only queen
whose bath I can see
whenever I like.

Let me explain.

I was walking my cat
(yes, my cat.
I'll tell you about him

another time)
in Greenwich Park
a week or so ago.

He was pulling
on the lead.

Frantically pulling.

Pulling so hard
I had no other choice
but to follow him.

I thought he had smelt
a rat.

He led me further and
further into the park
until we reached an outline
of an old palace.

Caroline of Brunswick
Queen Consort of the United Kingdom & Hanover, 1820 - 1821

George IV
King of the United Kingdom & Hanover, 1820 - 1830

He stopped
right there
and began cleaning his fur.

I looked at the ruins
of the old, old palace.

There, in one of the rooms,
was a bath.
It had steps leading
down into it,
beneath the ground.

The bath was gigantic.
Much bigger than my
little tub, which I
barely fit into.

I could swim lengths
in this bath.

(I was a little
bit jealous of it.)

When I got home
with Oscar, my cat,
I read about Queen Caroline.

When she left her
husband – King George IV –
he ordered his men
to raze her house
to the ground.

The men took his instructions
and as the bath
was built below the floor
they left it.

I liked Queen Caroline
and her bath.

I wonder if she had
any rubber ducks?

Like A Sun

Elli Woollard

Imagine. It's daybreak. You're only eighteen,
and somebody says 'Now it's time to be queen.'
You stir in your blankets. Who *was* it that spoke?
You're still half asleep. Was it some sort of joke?

Queen? I mean, *really*? You're dreaming it, right?
Then the curtains are opened, and in that faint light
stands your mother, who says 'Now, there's no time to dress',
so you get out of bed, with your hair still a mess,

and you walk down the cold empty length of the hall
all alone in the world, feeling lost and as small
as a pinprick star in the black of the sky.
   But a queen, like a sun, must be born, by and by.

···········

Victoria
Queen of the United Kingdom, 1837 - 1901

I know who you are, though I'm long since dead.
I've seen all you've done, and I've heard all you've said.
So I guess now you're chatting, or playing with apps,
or reading, or singing, or dancing, perhaps,

and your life's like a promise, a blank new page
that is open and free, not a palace-shaped cage.
You can learn, you can earn, be with friends, stay up late.
Not burdened at birth by some pre-decreed fate,

or bound by the coils of the old golden chain
of honour and duty and history, to reign.
I have to accept, but I want to scream 'WHY?'
    Yet a queen, like a sun, must rise, by and by.

Imagine. They tell you your uncle has died.
He was old, he was ill, but you're crying inside,
not only for him, but your childhood too,
and all of those things that you wanted to do.

There is so much in life that you don't understand,
so how will you manage to rule the whole land?
Meet ministers, lords… can't this wait? Not today.
You're still far too young! Oh, but what can you say?

So you put on a smile, and you tidy your frown.
You watch as the people around you bow down,
then you take up the crown, and you hold your head high.
    For a queen, like a sun, must blaze, by and by.

Early one morning, shortly after she turned eighteen, the young Victoria was woken by her mother. Still in her dressing gown, she made her way alone to greet the Archbishop of Canterbury and the Lord Chamberlain, who informed her that her uncle the king had died and she was now queen.

During Victoria's reign and that of her predecessor, William IV, many political movements arose demanding reform to the way the country was governed.

Some wanted to do away with the monarchy altogether. Most wanted, at the very least, for more people to have a vote on who represented them in Parliament.

Women still could not vote at this time, and though Britain now had a female ruler, Victoria was personally opposed to women's suffrage.

Queen Victoria's Twitter Feed

Elli Woollard

OMG! I've turned eighteen!
And now they've gone and made me queen!

Met this German guy named Bertie.
(Heart emoji.) Getting flirty!

Hey, I'm married! All in white.
Had twelve bridesmaids. What a sight!

Urgh! I'm preggers! Feel like cow.
Guess I'll be a mother now.

NINE kids now, including one
I don't much like (my eldest son).

Albert's died. I want him back.
So now I'm always wearing black.

They've made me Empress (hashtag: cool).
Just look at all the states I rule!

Today's my Golden Jubilee.
A public party, all for me!

Now been ruling SIXTY years.
Cheering crowds. I'm moved to tears.

(Waving hands.) My life is done.
But oh it's been a lot of fun!

Victoria hated being pregnant and thought that babies looked like frogs.

Her son Bertie, the future Edward VII, was a disappointment to his parents. Victoria blamed Bertie for her beloved Albert's death, because it was after a stressful visit to Bertie that Albert became ill.

In this period, the British Empire was at its height. Many countries around the world had been gradually taken over by British colonisers, including India. Victoria's Prime Minister, Benjamin Disraeli, proposed that this should be reflected in her title, and so Victoria was declared "Empress of India". After a long struggle, India became an independent nation again in 1947.

In the early 20th century, divorce was still often seen as scandalous – especially for the royal family. When King Edward told the Prime Minister he intended to marry a woman who was in the process of getting divorced from another man, Parliament decided they couldn't allow the King to marry a divorcee.

The Prince and the Beauty

(in the style of 'The Owl and the Pussycat')

Rebecca Colby

The Prince and the Beauty fell in love:
Edward and Wallis Simpson.
But the couple were harried, for she was still married,
and mulled over what could be done.
They pondered and pondered for many a day,
till they realised their only recourse –
said the Prince to his Beauty, 'O Wallis, my love,
it's best that you get a divorce,
divorce,
divorce.
It's best that you get a divorce.'

Edward VIII
King of the United Kingdom, June 1936 - December 1936

134

Then Wallis retorted, 'It's easily sorted,
just buy me a gold wedding ring.'
To which he replied, 'You'll soon be my bride
and stand by my side when I'm king.'
But their love was a scandal the crown couldn't handle
and the kingdom refused to condone.
So given a choice between Beauty and Duty,
he abdicated the throne,
the throne,
the throne.
He abdicated the throne.

He said, 'There's a cost, but all is not lost.
Let's move to a chateau in France.
We'll live out our days far removed from the gaze
of those who oppose our romance.'
Denied coronation, exiled from his nation,
apart from his family for life –
these hardships he bore, to make his heart soar
to remain with his true love: his wife,
his wife,
his wife.
To remain with his true love: his wife.

Rather than calling off the marriage, he decided to abdicate: he stepped down and left the throne to his brother. This romantic story remains popular.

Historians have a less rosy view of Edward, though, because he is often considered to have been a sympathiser with Nazi Germany.

First Day at School

Laura Mucha

I stare out of tinted windows
>   *He stares out of tinted windows*

as we roll closer and closer
>   *as we roll closer and closer*

to the red bricks and black gate.
>   *to the dreaded clicks of the cameras that wait.*

Dad opens the door and takes my hand.
>   *I open the door and take his hand.*

My feet feel heavy on the concrete.
>   *My heart is heavy. I feel it beat*

I count the steps... Clump clump clump.
>   *and bounce in my chest... Thump thump thump.*

'Welcome, Prince George,' the teacher says.
>   *'Welcome, Prince George,' the teacher says.*

We walk through the door, and I leave
>   *We walk through the door, and I breathe*

the *cha-cha-cha chaah* of cameras behind me.
>   *ahhhhhhhh. Privacy. Finally.*

···

Prince George of Cambridge

136

Royal figures have always been closely examined and widely discussed. Modern technology means we can do this even more easily now: but at what cost? In 1997, Princess Diana – Prince William's mother – died after being pursued through a tunnel by press photographers.

Now that the royal family have less actual power over Parliament's decisions, many news outlets treat them more like celebrities. The role and purpose of a royal family in Britain in the twenty-first century remains a subject of spirited debate.

Now for some

BONUS BITS

Interview with a historian: Dr Kate Wiles

After working on this book and enjoying investigating all these historical characters, we wanted to find out more from a professional historian.

Editor Rachel Piercey asked a historian she admires, Dr Kate Wiles, some questions about her job and her love of history.

★ **Can you tell us a bit about what you do?**

I'm an Anglo-Saxon historian, which means I try to understand England as it was before the Norman Conquest in 1066. But I also work at a history magazine, so I read about all kinds of history from around the world.

This week I've been reading about robots in Ancient Greece, the suffragettes, the First World War and Snoopy.

★ **What's the best thing about being a historian?**

It's like being a detective – following clues to try and understand people and their lives. By piecing little things together, we can see what someone a thousand years ago thought and felt, what they liked to wear and eat and do, how they spoke, where they went and who they loved. Sometimes it's like reading a story or watching a film, but it was real.

★ **Who is the monarch you'd most like to meet and what would you ask them?**

Elizabeth I, I think. We know so much about her but there's so much we don't know. I'd want to follow her around for a day and ask her a million annoying questions about tiny everyday things – not about affairs of state, but about *her*.

★ **Is there any one king or queen who is generally considered to have been particularly good?**

It depends what you think being a good king or queen means. Victoria is considered a good queen, for example, but as Britain got more powerful (and it really did), lots of people suffered. And how great was Alfred the Great, actually? He lost half of England to the Vikings!

★ **What about particularly bad?**

Bad King John was pretty bad and his people hated him, but because of him Magna Carta was written and it changed what powers we thought it was acceptable for a monarch to have. Richard III wasn't great though…

★ **Who is your favourite king or queen?**

I love Queen Emma. She hasn't got a poem in this book, which is fine, because she never ruled. But she was wife to King Æthelred and then Cnut, and she was the mother of Edward the Confessor and Harthacnut. Through her, England, Denmark, Norway and Normandy were connected. She lived through dramatic times and a lot of upheaval, and was an incredibly powerful woman.

140

★   Do you have a favourite poem in *The Head that Wears a Crown?*

I couldn't pick just one! They're as different and clever and silly and sad and beautiful as the kings and queens they're about.

★   What would you recommend to a young person interested in becoming a historian?

Follow your nose. Read about what you love, even if it's not about history, because it will all end up being useful. I studied languages first because that's what I loved when I was younger. The languages I studied got older and older until I was studying manuscripts, and then I started following the clues in them to find out about who wrote them and who read them and realised I was a historian. Follow your nose!

★   ★   ★

Dr Kate Wiles is Senior Editor of *History Today* and an Anglo-Saxonist. She researches the history of how people spoke and wrote multiple languages and is the historical language consultant for the TV drama *Vikings*. She loves manuscripts, lasagne, ancient languages and old maps.

Write your own poem

Fancy writing your own poem and then maybe illustrating it too? Editor Rachel Piercey has come up with some ideas to help get you started.

★ Like Henry VII and his monkey, many kings and queens throughout history have kept pets and exotic animals: Henry I had lions, leopards, camels and porcupines; George III was given a cheetah; Queen Victoria owned a donkey, a parrot and several doted-on dogs; Princess Elizabeth and Princess Margaret were gifted pet chameleons. Indeed, the Queen is now well-known for her love of corgis.

 **Research a historical pet (or make one up!) and write a poem from the animal's point of view.** What is their life like at court? Do they enjoy the luxury of being a royal pet or do they long for freedom? What do they think of the king or queen's interest in riches and power?

★ In 'A Nice Cup of Tea and a Sit Down', Anna shows that there are often two sides to a historical story. **Choose a famous historical event or figure and write a two-stanza poem, exploring opposite viewpoints on the same subject.** How will you lay out your poem?

★ **Imagine that you have just been made the ruler of a new kingdom.** What will be your first law? How will you celebrate your coronation and how will you decorate your throne room, the seat of your power? How does it feel to have so much power so suddenly?

★ **Write a list poem of laws you would make if you were a monarch.** Aim for a mixture: rules for a fairer world; fanciful, magical laws; laws which are highly personal to you as an individual.

Pick the law you think is most important and choose a way to highlight its significance – you might say that it's the first law you will pass, or you might repeat the words of this law, or put them in capital letters.

★ Dr Kate Wiles loves Queen Emma, but Queen Emma doesn't have a poem in this book! Can you write one?

Do some research into Emma's life and pick a few of your favourite facts. But don't just tell us about these life events – show them in action.

★ **Choose an Anglo-Saxon monarch and write an alliterating poem about them, in the style of an Old English poem.** For each line, choose a new letter and find as many words as you can that begin with it.

Divide each line in two, with at least four syllables in each half and a gap in the middle.

★ In 'John, (Not Quite) King of England', Rachael repeats the word 'royal' in almost every line, to create a sense of John's obsession with becoming king.

Choose a word that is connected to regal power and write a poem where you use it as much as possible, to reveal what's on your monarch's mind.

★ Pick two monarchs from different times and write a poem where they meet each other.

What do they have in common? What do they find strange, or what do they argue about? Are they wearing similar clothes? Do they jostle for power?

★ Anna and Richard have both written shape poems, to reflect the hobbies of Elizabeth of York and George III.

Choose a monarch, and an item which was important to them, and write a poem in its shape.

We'd love to see what you come up with in response to these prompts! If you'd like us to take a look, email your poems and pictures to hello@theemmapress.com with 'The Head that Wears a Crown' in the subject line.

About the editors

Rachel Piercey is a poet and editor for adults and children. She regularly performs her poems and runs writing workshops at schools and festivals across the country. Rachel's poems have appeared in *The Rialto, Magma, Poems in Which, Butcher's Dog* and *The Poetry Review*, as well as various Emma Press pamphlets and anthologies, and in 2008 she won the Newdigate Prize. She lives in London. rachelpierceypoet.com

Emma Dai'an Wright is a British-Chinese-Vietnamese publisher, designer and illustrator based in Birmingham, UK. She studied Classics at Brasenose College, Oxford, and worked in ebook production at Orion Publishing Group before leaving in 2012 to set up the Emma Press with the support of the Prince's Trust.

About the poets

Aileen Ballantyne is the former staff medical correspondent for the *Guardian* and the *Sunday Time*s and her investigative journalism has twice been commended in the British Press Awards. Aileen has a PhD in Creative Writing and Modern Poetry from Edinburgh University, where she now teaches Literature and Contemporary Poetry.

Meghan Ballard was adopted from South Korea, but now lives in the Rocky Mountains of Utah with her husband and two young children. As a child, she was sure she was misplaced royalty, but to her dismay, they have yet to come claim her. This is her first published poem.

Jerrold Bowam is a British/Canadian writer who aspires to find others who are as amused as his muse, have a predilection for repetition and a penchant for recurrence.

Melanie Branton writes and performs both funny and serious poems. She has worked as an English and Drama teacher and as an assistant theatre director, but has, sadly, never been a queen. Her poetry collections for adults are *My Cloth-Eared Heart* (Oversteps, 2017) and *Can You See Where I'm Coming From?* (Burning Eye, 2018).

Carole Bromley was shortlisted for the 2014 Manchester Writing for Children Award and her poem 'Goldilocks' was performed at the CLiPPA Awards in 2015. She was highly commended in the Caterpillar Competition 2016 and her first collection for children, *Blast Off!*, was published by Smith Doorstop in 2017.

Jane Burn spent her childhood wrapping bath-towel capes around herself while wearing tin-foil crowns. She thinks kings and queens are fascinating – there are so many of them and most have done some very odd, fascinating, terrible or wonderful stuff. They are well worth learning about.

John Canfield grew up in Cornwall and now tries not to be a grown up in London. He writes poems and sometimes people put them in books and sometimes they don't. A promising career as a clown was scuppered by his desire to grow a beard.

Mary Anne Clark studies English at Merton College, Oxford, where she won the 2016 Newdigate Prize. Her poems have appeared in *ASH, The Mays, The Kindling* and two Emma Press children's poetry anthologies.

Rebecca Colby taught English in Taiwan, worked for a Russian comedian and travelled the world as a tour director before writing books and poems for children. Her books include *There was a Wee Lassie who Swallowed a Midgie, It's Raining Bats & Frogs, Motor Goose* and *Captain Bling's Christmas Plunder*.

Shauna Darling Robertson's poems for adults and children have been performed by actors, set to music, displayed on buses, made into comic art, hung on a pub wall and published in a bunch of books and magazines. She has two chapbooks, *Blueprints for a Minefield* (Fair Acre Press, 2016) and *Love Bites* (Dancing Girl Press, 2018).

Dharmavadana is fascinated by history, and living in London he feels surrounded by it. He has written several historical poems and one story set in the Middle Ages, about a knight, a monk and twin monsters. He has a (non-historical) poem in the Emma Press anthology *Watcher of the Skies: Poems about Space and Aliens*.

Julie Anna Douglas lives on the West Coast of Scotland. Her poetry has appeared in *Spider* and *Ember* magazines in USA and in *The Caterpillar* in Ireland, and her poem 'Recipe for Cosmic Cupcakes' featured in *Watcher of the Skies: Poems about Space and Aliens*. She is a writer for *Amazing Children's Educational Magazine*.

Matthew Haigh lives and works in Cardiff. His poems have appeared in *Poetry London, Poetry Wales, Magma* and the *Guardian*. He has also contributed to the Sidekick Books anthology *Coin Opera II: Fulminare's Revenge*, a book of poems inspired by computer games.

Jack Houston lives in London with his wife and two young sons. He works in Hackney's public libraries where he holds free poetry workshops that you (yes, you) are welcome to too. He likes playing the drums for his band, Bugeye, and walking Raffles, his very silly dog.

Kirsten Irving lives in London and is the joint ruler of Sidekick Books. She has minimal conquests to her name, but counts among her titles High Priestess of Crows and Devourer of Books. @KoftheTriffids

Anna Kisby is a poet and mother of three living in Devon. She's loved history ever since seeing Tudor graffiti in Queen Elizabeth I's cell in the Tower of London on a school trip. She won the BBC Proms Poetry competition 2016 and has poems in various magazines and anthologies.

David McKelvie lives at the top of a hill in Greenock, Scotland. Each day, he passes Dumbarton Rock, once home to the now forgotten kingdom of Alt Clut. All his poems are written to be heard by children.

Emma Rose Millar writes historical fiction for adults and poetry for children. Her novel *Five Guns Blazing* was first place category winner in The Chaucer Awards for Historical Fiction. Her novella, *The Women Friends: Selina* was shortlisted for the Goethe Award in 2016. She has recently published her third novel, *Delirium* with Crooked Cat Books.

Fiona Mills wrote lots of poems and stories when she was at school, but stopped when she grew up and became a journalist. Now she has three children of her own, she has starting making things up again. Queen Anne's Lace is the first of her poems to be published.

Brian Moses has been a professional poet/writer-in-schools/anthologist/percussionist since 1988. He has published over 200 books and his Macmillan poetry books have sold over a million copies. He is featured on the Poetry Archive. His latest book is *Lost Magic: The Very Best of Brian Moses* (Macmillan).

Laura Mucha studied flying trapeze, philosophy and psychology, and swam in Antarctica before becoming a lawyer. Now she's a full time poet, author and performer. She won the Caterpillar Poetry Prize, Poetry Ireland featured her as one of eight poets displayed on the Dublin overground, and her debut book is *Love Factually* (Bloomsbury).

Alan Murphy has written lots of strange poems for children and teenagers, which he usually illustrates with his own colourful collages. His books *Prometheus Unplugged* and *Psychosilly* were shortlisted for the Irish CAP awards. His latest collection is *All Gums Blazing*. He lives in West Waterford and is not mad.

Rachael M Nicholas is a poet from Birmingham. In 2012 she was lucky enough to win the Eric Gregory Award. Her poems in previous Emma

Press anthologies have been about space (very big!), the Minotaur (very scary!) and Ariadne (very, very clever!).

Richard O'Brien is a poet, translator and academic based in Birmingham, UK. He has a PhD on Shakespeare and the development of verse drama. Richard's pamphlets include *The Emmores* (Emma Press, 2014) and *A Bloody Mess* (Valley Press, 2015). In 2017, he won an Eric Gregory Award from the Society of Authors for his poetry.

Suzanne Olivante's grandmother worked in service to Queen Elizabeth the Queen Mother in London and Balmoral Castle, spending hours polishing oodles of copper saucepans. Suzanne's poems have been published in several anthologies for children, placed in competitions and she was shortlisted for the National Literacy Trust Poetry Prize in 2015.

Catherine Olver is studying for a PhD in children's literature at the University of Cambridge. Katherine Parr has been her historical heroine since she played Katherine in a Year 5 play. Her drama teacher said he chose her for the part because she sits up straight, like a queen. She hopes her poem in this book will atone for her dreadful acting.

Kate O'Neil lives on the Northern Illawarra coast of NSW, Australia. Her poems for children have been published in magazines and anthologies including *The Caterpillar* and *Let in the Stars*. She was shortlisted for the 2014 Manchester Poetry for Children prize and her collection, *Cool Poems* will be published by Triple D Books in 2018.

John H Rice teaches, assesses and writes all sorts of educational materials. Sometimes he is afflicted by poetry and he has to write the poems down to stop them pinging around his head. He lives very near to where King Sweyn is rumoured to have moored his fleet.

Catherine Rockwood studied early-modern literature and history at St. Andrews, and Yale University. She lives in Massachusetts with her family, and hopes Owen, Iris and Tobias may enjoy this collection of poetry.

Toby Sligo lives with his wife and cat by the sea. When he is not reading or writing, he enjoys long country walks. This is his first published poem.

Jennifer Watson went on a spot of leave from the Cabinet Office, acquired two dogs and forgot to go back. She has been shortlisted for the Bridport Prize, the Wasafiri New Writing Prize and the Manchester Writing For Children Prize. Jennifer lives in a small village in Kent.

Jeremy Wikeley had an illustrated 'Kings and Queens of England' Ladybird book when he was a kid, and ended up studying History at university. These two things weren't unconnected. Jeremy works for the Orwell Foundation.

Kate Wise has been published in various Emma Press anthologies, and journals including the *Rialto*, *Structo*, and *Poems in Which*. Despite owning several of those rulers from museums, she is yet to learn the order of the British Monarchs... She grew up in Cheshire, and tweets at @kwise62

Elli Woollard grew up thinking she was distantly related to royalty, only to discover that her ancestors had told massive fibs about their heritage. Like them, Elli likes telling stories, but she gets them published. The author of several picture books, she lives in London with her husband and four children.

Ros Woolner works as a translator from her home in Wolverhampton, which she shares with her partner, her two children and a black cat called Henry who likes to walk across laptops and sit on paper.

About the Emma Press

The Emma Press is an independent publishing house based in the Jewellery Quarter, Birmingham, UK. We specialise in poetry, short fiction and children's books.

The Emma Press won the Michael Marks Award for Poetry Pamphlet Publishers in 2016 and Emma Press books have won the Poetry Book Society Pamphlet Choice Award, the Saboteur Award for Best Collaborative Work, and CLiPPA, the CLPE award for children's poetry books.

We publish themed poetry anthologies, single-author poetry and fiction pamphlets (chapbooks), and books for children. We have a growing list of translations which includes titles from Latvia, Estonia, Indonesia, Spain and the Netherlands.

We run regular calls for submissions, and try to do as many events as possible, from book-launch parties to writing workshops to school visits.

You can find out more about the Emma Press and buy books directly from us here:

theemmapress.com

Once Upon A Time In Birmingham
Women Who Dared To Dream

Stories by Louise Palfreyman
Illustrations by Jan Bowman, Yasmin Bryan,
Amy Louise Evans, Saadia Hipkiss, Chein Shyan Lee,
Farah Osseili & Michelle Turton

Who was the world's first female programmer? Who made history as the first British woman to sail solo around the world non-stop? Who is Birmingham's first female Muslim MP? Meet Mary Lee Berners-Lee, Lisa Clayton, Shabana Mahmood and many more in Once Upon a Time in Birmingham, a lively introduction to thirty of Birmingham's most awe-inspiring women, past and present.

From pioneers in their field to everyday heroines, these are women who refused to be silenced, who fought for what they believed in, who proved they were just as good as men... if not better!

£14.99
Hardback ISBN 978-1-910139-82-0
Stories about real-life women aimed at children aged 11+

ALSO FROM THE EMMA PRESS

Everyone's the Smartest

Poems by Contra, illustrated by Ulla Saar
Translated from Estonian by Charlotte Geater,
Kätlin Kaldmaa & Richard O'Brien

School can be hard, fun and strange – sometimes all at once. It's full of your best friends and all the teachers as well as lots of kids you haven't met. Every day reveals more stories and challenges…

Everyone's the Smartest is a collection of poems which tell strange new stories in familiar settings. From clever ducks who fly far away while children are stuck in school, to bathroom taps that are just one mistake away from turning the school into a great lake, this collection reminds its readers that there is wonder everywhere.

£12.00
Paperback ISBN 978-1-910139-99-8
Poems aimed at children aged 8+

The Book of Clouds

**Poems by Juris Kronbergs, illustrated by Anete Melece
Translated from Latvian by Mara Rozitis & Richard O'Brien.**

If you look up on a cloudy day, you'll see a whole new surprising world above you – the world of clouds! *The Book of Clouds* is an introduction to this world – and the guide you'll want by your side to help you understand it.

A mix of dreamy fantasy and scientific fact, this is the perfect gift for any child with their head stuck in the clouds – and for anyone who has ever wondered what's up there in the skies above. This book is ideal for children to use as a starting point for their own imaginative creative play.

With 25 poems and many full-page illustrations that use watercolour and collage, you won't be able to pick *The Book of Clouds* up without wanting to immediately start making your own cloud diary.

£12.00
Hardback ISBN 978-1-910139-14-1
Poems aimed at children aged 8+

ALSO FROM THE EMMA PRESS

The Dog Who Found Sorrow

A story by Rūta Briede
Illustrated by Elīna Brasliņa
Translated from Latvian by Elīna Brasliņa

An entire city is suddenly enveloped in black clouds of sorrow that rob everything of colour and scent. A brave dog decides to resist the sadness and climbs up into the big cloud of sorrow to find out what's hiding up there – and to make it go away.

The Dog Who Found Sorrow is a poetic picture book for children and adults alike – a story about the power of emotions.

£10.00
Hardback ISBN 978-1-910139-54-7
A picture book aimed at children aged 4+

The Noisy Classroom

**Poems by Ieva Samauska, illustrated by Vivianna Maria Staņislavska
Translated by Žanete Vēvere Pasqualini,
Sara Smith and Richard O'Brien**

It isn't easy being a kid – especially not in the noisiest class in the school. Some days, you struggle with algebra, or too much homework. Sometimes, one of your fellow pupils just won't SHUT UP. When the class feels like a many-headed dragon, how can you find a place for yourself? Would you feel less lonely if you could smuggle a cat in?

The Noisy Classroom features poems which tackle social anxiety and the pressures of modern life on children, capturing familiar feelings of loneliness and being overworked. The book features bonus materials at the end. These give the reader an insight into the life of the writer and the illustrator, and encourage them to write and draw themselves.

£8.50
Hardback ISBN 978-1-910139-82-0
Poems aimed at children aged 8+